Auto Body — 5S Audit Review Form

Date: _____   Evaluation Area: _____

5S Element	Number	Evaluation Criteria	Rank these items from 1 through 5: 5 being well done	Score (1-5)	Ideas / Suggestions / Comments
SORT	I	Are the aisles and walkways open and clear?	All items that are not necessary or unsafe have been removed from the area where people travel and work.		
	II	Is the work area free of any spills of fluids?	Consider whether there are any lubricants, water, oils or other materials that may be hazardous in the work area, on the floor, or under vehicles that are not necessary.		
	III	Is the work area free of unnecessary items and tools?	Are items that are not needed been removed from the work zone, i.e. tools, parts, cans, tags, extra items.		
	IV	Is the work area free of excess consumables/materials?	Evaluate against how many items are in the work area. Assess if the materials, parts, and supplies are currently needed for the repair area, staging area, point area, etc.		
	V	Is the production/ information board active and to what degree?	All jobs in each respective area of the shop are known and displayed. Announcements are current and in presentable shape. Arrangement is straight and placed under appropriate headings.		
	VI	Are the area's walls and dividers free of items not used in the shop?	Extra items are not on the walls, dividers, or hanging of signs that are not necessary.		
		Category Subtotal		- - - - - -	
		Sort Score: Subtotal divided by 6			
SET IN ORDER / STRAIGHTEN	VII	Evaluate any documentation storage.	Only documents to do the job are stored at the work area. Stock is limited and pre-staging is based on known lead-times throughput of the repair shop. Documentation is understandable to outsiders.		
	VIII	How are the shelves, desks, and work surfaces arranged?	All locations of items are labeled, marked, and it is known if they are missing.		
	IX	How are the tools and material used in operations stored?	No items are resting on or under automobiles nor tucked in corners. No items are resting on essential equipment, unknown in cupboards, or other places.		
	X	Evaluate temporary storage containers and staging locations and tidiness.	Parts, re-manufactured, components, and other items are stored in the appropriate place and orientated well for specific stage of the repair process. Items are secure and not causing any danger to the works.		
	XI	Assess orderliness of items on the shop's floor.	Minimal items are sitting directly on the floor and no materials are left around the vehicles. Items that need to be set on the floor are clearly marked and positioned in designated areas clearly outlined.		
	XII	Availability of tools for repair and teardown as well as measuring gauges.	Tools, components, measuring devices, and any fixtures need for teardown and repair are organized in a systematic way to ensure they are easily within reach and if not available are known where they are.		
		Category Subtotal		- - - - - -	
		Set in Order / Straighten Score: Subtotal divided by 6			
SHINE / SWEEP	XIII	The storage of gauges and tooling.	Arrangement and storage of all fixtures, tools, and gauges are kept in clean well organized and visual area for storage and no risk of damage or loss can occur.		
	XIV	Clear when equipment needs maintenance and when last maintained.	Machines are clearly marked, highlighted, and labeled. Compliance or check sheets are clean and displayed. Any maintenance is known scheduled; fluid levels, lubrication, and joints are accessible.		
	XV	In each department assess the cleanliness of the work area.	How dust free are the areas. Look under equipment, under vehicles, behind work benches, and tool chests to see if there is garbage and other unnecessary items.		
	XVI	Safety, are areas sectioned off and safe for workers?	Spray shields and physical guards are in active use to keep paint overspray and other sprays within the department. How much paint is getting on the floor. All critical areas are clearly marked to protect workers.		
	XVII	Assess status of equipment in the area. Cleanliness overall appearance.	Are machines, repair equipment, and other vehicles known to be on a maintenance schedule for cleaning and repair?		
		Category Subtotal		- - - - - -	
		Shine / Sweep Score: Subtotal divided by 5			
STANDARDIZE	XVIII	Is there visual color diagramming and color coding?	A clear and present color coding system is present in the work areas and across the shop. It's immediately clear that standards are being maintained and improved on.		
	XIX	Assess the access ways in case of emergency.	All emergency systems; fire vehicles, fire extinguishers, and emergency equipment free of obstruction and clear at all times. Access to electrical controls and fuses are known, marked, and free of any obstructions.		
	XX	The aisle ways are bright with light and clearly marked.	Walkways are clearly highlighted for direction, aisle access identified at any moment while in the work area. Transitional areas between the different departments and intersections are clearly marked.		
	XXI	General area has quantity limits for stored parts and are marked clearly.	Heights are marked, quantity of materials are known, and min vs. max is maintained. Shop carts are standardized to hold only parts for one vehicle. Large parts are clearly related to their respective cart.		
	XXII	Is there clear document control of information in the work zone?	All information and documentation is controlled, labeled, and revisions are up to date. There are no label-less binders or work orders in the area.		
		Category Subtotal		- - - - - -	
		Standardize Score: Subtotal divided by 5			
SUSTAIN	XXIII	The aisle ways are clean and maintenance is clear.	Aisles are never full of anything and are clear for passage. All vehicle parts are stored in work areas and only in designated storage areas next to aisles therefore allowing accessible movement in the area.		
	XXIV	Illustrations and work area plans are available to compare against.	5S operates a system that allows for controlled change and further improvement of 5S in the work areas. Scoring is kept on each of these 5's and history is present and visible to support future improvement.		
	XXV	Organization is now visible. Tool locations are known and allocated.	No self-discipline is necessary to ensure that all tools, equipment, gauges, and parts are put back in the same spot. No extra effort is needed to sustain 5S in the area.		
	XXVI	Evaluate the involvement of supervisors in 5S.	Supervisors are actively involved in the review process of 5S and are supporting improvement activities of the work areas.		
		Category Subtotal		- - - - - -	
		Sustain Score: Subtotal divided by 4			

Total "Category Subtotals" divide by 26 average 5S score: TOTAL [_ _ _ _]

Auto Body — 5S Audit Review Form

Date: _____   Evaluation Area: _____

5S Element	Number	Evaluation Criteria	Rank these items from 1 through 5: 5 being well done	Score (1-5)	Ideas / Suggestions / Comments
SORT	I	Are the aisles and walkways open and clear?	All items that are not necessary or unsafe have been removed from the area where people travel and work.		
	II	Is the work area free of any spills of fluids?	Consider whether there are any lubricants, water, oils or other materials that may be hazardous in the work area, on the floor, or under vehicles that are not necessary.		
	III	Is the work area free of unnecessary items and tools?	Are items that are not needed been removed from the work zone, i.e. tools, parts, cans, tags, extra items.		
	IV	Is the work area free of excess consumables/materials?	Evaluate against how many items are in the work area. Assess if the materials, parts, and supplies are currently needed for the repair area, staging area, point area, etc.		
	V	Is the production/ information board active and to what degree?	All jobs in each respective area of the shop are known and displayed. Announcements are current and in presentable shape. Arrangement is straight and placed under appropriate headings.		
	VI	Are the area's walls and dividers free of items not used in the shop?	Extra items are not on the walls, dividers, or hanging of signs that are not necessary.		

Category Subtotal ....

Sort Score: Subtotal divided by 6

5S Element	Number	Evaluation Criteria	Rank these items from 1 through 5: 5 being well done	Score (1-5)	Ideas / Suggestions / Comments
SET IN ORDER / STRAIGHTEN	VII	Evaluate any documentation storage.	Only documents to do the job are stored at the work area. Stock is limited and pre-staging is based on known lead-times throughout of the repair shop. Documentation is understandable to outsiders.		
	VIII	How are the shelves, desks, and work surfaces arranged?	All locations of items are labeled, marked, and it is known if they are missing.		
	IX	How are the tools and material used in operations stored?	No items are resting on or under automobiles nor tucked in corners. No items are resting on essential equipment, unknown in cupboards, or other places.		
	X	Evaluate temporary storage containers and staging locations and tidiness.	Parts, re-manufactured, components, and other items are stored in the appropriate place and orientated well for specific stage of the repair process. Items are secure and not causing any danger to the works.		
	XI	Assess orderliness of items on the shop's floor.	Minimal items are sitting directly on the floor and no materials are left around the vehicles. Items that need to be set on the floor are clearly marked and positioned in designated areas clearly outlined.		
	XII	Availability of tools for repair and teardown as well as measuring gauges.	Tools, components, measuring devices, and any fixtures need for teardown and repair are organized in a systematic way to ensure they are easily within reach and if not available are known where they are.		

Category Subtotal ....

Set in Order / Straighten Score: Subtotal divided by 6

5S Element	Number	Evaluation Criteria	Rank these items from 1 through 5: 5 being well done	Score (1-5)	Ideas / Suggestions / Comments
SHINE / SWEEP	XIII	The storage of gauges and tooling.	Arrangement and storage of all fixtures, tools, and gauges are kept in clean well organized and visual area for storage and no risk of damage or loss can occur.		
	XIV	Clear when equipment needs maintenance and when last maintained.	Machines are clearly marked, highlighted, and labeled. Compliance or check sheets are clean and displayed. Any maintenance is known scheduled; fluid levels, lubrication, and joints are accessible.		
	XV	In each department assess the cleanliness of the work area.	How dust free are the areas. Look under equipment, under vehicles, behind work benches, and tool chests to see if there is garbage and other unnecessary items.		
	XVI	Safety, are areas sectioned off and safe for workers?	Spray shields and physical guards are in active use to keep paint overspray and other sprays within the department. How much paint is getting on the floor. All critical areas are clearly marked to protect workers.		
	XVII	Assess status of equipment in the area. Cleanliness overall appearance.	Are machines, repair equipment, and other vehicles known to be on a maintenance schedule for cleaning and repair?		

Category Subtotal ....

Shine / Sweep Score: Subtotal divided by 5

5S Element	Number	Evaluation Criteria	Rank these items from 1 through 5: 5 being well done	Score (1-5)	Ideas / Suggestions / Comments
STANDARDIZE	XVIII	Is there visual color diagramming and color coding?	A clear and present color coding system is present in the work areas and across the shop. It's immediately clear that standards are being maintained and improved on.		
	XIX	Assess the access ways in case of emergency.	All emergency systems; fire vehicles, fire extinguishers, and emergency equipment free of obstruction and clear at all times. Access to electrical controls and fuses are known, marked, and free of any obstructions.		
	XX	The aisle ways are bright with light and clearly marked.	Walkways are clearly highlighted for direction, aisle access identified at any moment while in the work area. Transitional areas between the different departments and intersections are clearly marked.		
	XXI	General area has quantity limits for stored parts and are marked clearly.	Heights are marked, quantity of materials are known, and min vs. max is maintained. Shop carts are standardized to hold only parts for one vehicle. Large parts are clearly related to their respective cart.		
	XXII	Is there clear document control of information in the work zone?	All information and documentation is controlled, labeled, and revisions are up to date. There are no label-less binders or work orders in the area.		

Category Subtotal ....

Standardize Score: Subtotal divided by 5

5S Element	Number	Evaluation Criteria	Rank these items from 1 through 5: 5 being well done	Score (1-5)	Ideas / Suggestions / Comments
SUSTAIN	XXIII	The aisle ways are clean and maintenance is clear.	Aisles are never full of anything and are clear for passage. All vehicle parts are stored in work areas and only in designated storage areas next to aisles therefore allowing accessible movement in the area.		
	XXIV	Illustrations and work area plans are available to compare against.	5S operates a system that allows for controlled change and further improvement of 5S in the work areas. Scoring is kept on each of these 5's and history is present and visible to support future improvement.		
	XXV	Organization is now visible. Tool locations are known and allocated.	No self-discipline is necessary to ensure that all tools, equipment, gauges, and parts are put back in the same spot. No extra effort is needed to sustain 5S in the area.		
	XXVI	Evaluate the involvement of supervisors in 5S.	Supervisors are actively involved in the review process of 5S and are supporting improvement activities of the work areas.		

Category Subtotal ....

Sustain Score: Subtotal divided by 4

Total "Category Subtotals" divide by 26 average 5S score: TOTAL [____]

Auto Body — 5S Audit Review Form

Date: _____   Evaluation Area: _____

5S Element	Number	Evaluation Criteria	Rank these items from 1 through 5: 5 being well done	Score (1-5)	Ideas / Suggestions / Comments
SORT	I	Are the aisles and walkways open and clear?	All items that are not necessary or unsafe have been removed from the area where people travel and work.		
	II	Is the work area free of any spills of fluids?	Consider whether there are any lubricants, water, oils or other materials that may be hazardous in the work area, on the floor, or under vehicles that are not necessary.		
	III	Is the work area free of unnecessary items and tools?	Are items that are not needed been removed from the work zone, i.e. tools, parts, cans, tags, extra items.		
	IV	Is the work area free of excess consumables/materials?	Evaluate against how many items are in the work area. Assess if the materials, parts, and supplies are currently needed for the repair area, staging area, point area, etc.		
	V	Is the production/ information board active and to what degree?	All jobs in each respective area of the shop are known and displayed. Announcements are current and in presentable shape. Arrangement is straight and placed under appropriate headings.		
	VI	Are the area's walls and dividers free of items not used in the shop?	Extra items are not on the walls, dividers, or hanging of signs that are not necessary.		
			Category Subtotal		
			Sort Score: Subtotal divided by 6		
SET IN ORDER / STRAIGHTEN	VII	Evaluate any documentation storage.	Only documents to do the job are stored at the work area. Stock is limited and pre-staging is based on known lead-times throughout the repair shop. Documentation is understandable to outsiders.		
	VIII	How are the shelves, desks, and work surfaces arranged?	All locations of items are labeled, marked, and it is known if they are missing.		
	IX	How are the tools and material used in operations stored?	No items are resting on or under automobiles nor tucked in corners. No items are resting on essential equipment, unknown in cupboards, or other places.		
	X	Evaluate temporary storage containers and staging locations and tidiness.	Parts, re-manufactured, components, and other items are stored in the appropriate place and orientated well for specific stage of the repair process. Items are secure and not causing any danger to the works.		
	XI	Assess orderliness of items on the shop's floor.	Minimal items are sitting directly on the floor and no materials are left around the vehicles. Items that need to be set on the floor are clearly marked and positioned in designated areas clearly outlined.		
	XII	Availability of tools for repair and teardown as well as measuring gauges.	Tools, components, measuring devices, and any fixtures need for teardown and repair are organized in a systematic way to ensure they are easily within reach and if not available are known where they are.		
			Category Subtotal		
			Set in Order / Straighten Score: Subtotal divided by 6		
SHINE / SWEEP	XIII	The storage of gauges and tooling.	Arrangement and storage of all fixtures, tools, and gauges are kept in clean well organized and visual area for storage and no risk of damage or loss can occur.		
	XIV	Clear when equipment needs maintenance and when last maintained.	Machines are clearly marked, highlighted, and labeled. Compliance or check sheets are clean and displayed. Any maintenance is known scheduled; fluid levels, lubrication, and joints are accessible.		
	XV	In each department assess the cleanliness of the work area.	How dust free are the areas. Look under equipment, under vehicles, behind work benches, and tool chests to see if there is garbage and other unnecessary items.		
	XVI	Safety, are areas sectioned off and safe for workers?	Spray shields and physical guards are in active use to keep paint overspray and other sprays within the department. How much paint is getting on the floor. All critical areas are clearly marked to protect workers.		
	XVII	Assess status of equipment in the area. Cleanliness overall appearance.	Are machines, repair equipment, and other vehicles known to be on a maintenance schedule for cleaning and repair?		
			Category Subtotal		
			Shine / Sweep Score: Subtotal divided by 5		
STANDARDIZE	XVIII	Is there visual color diagramming and color coding?	A clear and present color coding system is present in the work areas and across the shop. It's immediately clear that standards are being maintained and improved on.		
	XIX	Assess the access ways in case of emergency.	All emergency systems; fire vehicles, fire extinguishers, and emergency equipment free of obstruction and clear at all times. Access to electrical controls and fuses are known, marked, and free of any obstructions.		
	XX	The aisle ways are bright with light and clearly marked.	Walkways are clearly highlighted for direction, aisle access identified at any moment while in the work area. Transitional areas between the different departments and intersections are clearly marked.		
	XXI	General area has quantity limits for stored parts and are marked clearly.	Heights are marked, quantity of materials are known, and min vs. max is maintained. Shop carts are standardized to hold only parts for one vehicle. Large parts are clearly related to their respective cart.		
	XXII	Is there clear document control of information in the work zone?	All information and documentation is controlled, labeled, and revisions are up to date. There are no label-less binders or work orders in the area.		
			Category Subtotal		
			Standardize Score: Subtotal divided by 5		
SUSTAIN	XXIII	The aisle ways are clean and maintenance is clear.	Aisles are never full of anything and are clear for passage. All vehicle parts are stored in work areas and only in designated storage areas next to aisles therefore allowing accessible movement in the area.		
	XXIV	Illustrations and work area plans are available to compare against.	5S operates a system that allows for controlled change and further improvement of 5S in the work areas. Scoring is kept on each of these 5's and history is present and visible to support future improvement.		
	XXV	Organization is now visible. Tool locations are known and allocated.	No self-discipline is necessary to ensure that all tools, equipment, gauges, and parts are put back in the same spot. No extra effort is needed to sustain 5S in the area.		
	XXVI	Evaluate the involvement of supervisors in 5S.	Supervisors are actively involved in the review process of 5S and are supporting improvement activities of the work areas.		
			Category Subtotal		
			Sustain Score: Subtotal divided by 4		

Total "Category Subtotals" divide by 26 average 5S score: TOTAL [____]

Auto Body — 5S Audit Review Form

Date: _____   Evaluation Area: _____

5S Element	Number	Evaluation Criteria	Rank these items from 1 through 5: 5 being well done	Score (1-5)	Ideas / Suggestions / Comments
SORT	I	Are the aisles and walkways open and clear?	All items that are not necessary or unsafe have been removed from the area where people travel and work.		
	II	Is the work area free of any spills of fluids?	Consider whether there are any lubricants, water, oils or other materials that may be hazardous in the work area, on the floor, or under vehicles that are not necessary.		
	III	Is the work area free of unnecessary items and tools?	Are items that are not needed been removed from the work zone, i.e. tools, parts, cans, tags, extra items.		
	IV	Is the work area free of excess consumables/materials?	Evaluate against how many items are in the work area. Assess if the materials, parts, and supplies are currently needed for the repair area, staging area, point area, etc.		
	V	Is the production/ information board active and to what degree?	All jobs in each respective area of the shop are known and displayed. Announcements are current and in presentable shape. Arrangement is straight and placed under appropriate headings.		
	VI	Are the area's walls and dividers free of items not used in the shop?	Extra items are not on the walls, dividers, or hanging of signs that are not necessary.		
			Category Subtotal		
			Sort Score: Subtotal divided by 6		
SET IN ORDER / STRAIGHTEN	VII	Evaluate any documentation storage.	Only documents to do the job are stored at the work area. Stock is limited and pre-staging is based on known lead-times throughput of the repair shop. Documentation is understandable to outsiders		
	VIII	How are the shelves, desks, and work surfaces arranged?	All locations of items are labeled, marked, and it is known if they are missing.		
	IX	How are the tools and material used in operations stored?	No items are resting on or under automobiles nor tucked in corners. No items are resting on essential equipment, unknown in cupboards, or other places.		
	X	Evaluate temporary storage containers and staging locations and tidiness.	Parts, re-manufactured, components, and other items are stored in the appropriate place and orientated well for specific stage of the repair process. Items are secure and not causing any danger to the works.		
	XI	Assess orderliness of items on the shop's floor.	Minimal items are sitting directly on the floor and no materials are left around the vehicles. Items that need to be set on the floor are clearly marked and positioned in designated areas clearly outlined.		
	XII	Availability of tools for repair and teardown as well as measuring gauges.	Tools, components, measuring devices, and any fixtures need for teardown and repair are organized in a systematic way to ensure they are easily within reach and if not available are known where they are.		
			Category Subtotal		
			Set in Order / Straighten Score: Subtotal divided by 6		
SHINE / SWEEP	XIII	The storage of gauges and tooling.	Arrangement and storage of all fixtures, tools, and gauges are kept in clean well organized and visual area for storage and no risk of damage or loss can occur.		
	XIV	Clear when equipment needs maintenance and when last maintained.	Machines are clearly marked, highlighted, and labeled. Compliance or check sheets are clean and displayed. Any maintenance is known scheduled; fluid levels, lubrication, and joints are accessible.		
	XV	In each department assess the cleanliness of the work area.	How dust free are the areas. Look under equipment, under vehicles, behind work benches, and tool chests to see if there is garbage and other unnecessary items.		
	XVI	Safety, are areas sectioned off and safe for workers?	Spray shields and physical guards are in active use to keep paint overspray and other sprays within the department. How much paint is getting on the floor. All critical areas are clearly marked to protect workers.		
	XVII	Assess status of equipment in the area. Cleanliness overall appearance.	Are machines, repair equipment, and other vehicles known to be on a maintenance schedule for cleaning and repair?		
			Category Subtotal		
			Shine / Sweep Score: Subtotal divided by 5		
STANDARDIZE	XVIII	Is there visual color diagramming and color coding?	A clear and present color coding system is present in the work areas and across the shop. It's immediately clear that standards are being maintained and improved on.		
	XIX	Assess the access ways in case of emergency.	All emergency systems; fire vehicles, fire extinguishers, and emergency equipment free of obstruction and clear at all times. Access to electrical controls and fuses are known, marked, and free of any obstructions.		
	XX	The aisle ways are bright with light and clearly marked.	Walkways are clearly highlighted for direction, aisle access identified at any moment while in the work area. Transitional areas between the different departments and intersections are clearly marked.		
	XXI	General area has quantity limits for stored parts and are marked clearly.	Heights are marked, quantity of materials are known, and min vs. max is maintained. Shop carts are standardized to hold only parts for one vehicle. Large parts are clearly related to their respective cart.		
	XXII	Is there clear document control of information in the work zone?	All information and documentation is controlled, labeled, and revisions are up to date. There are no label-less binders or work orders in the area.		
			Category Subtotal		
			Standardize Score: Subtotal divided by 5		
SUSTAIN	XXIII	The aisle ways are clean and maintenance is clear.	Aisles are never full of anything and are clear for passage. All vehicle parts are stored in work areas and only in designated storage areas next to aisles therefore allowing accessible movement in the area.		
	XXIV	Illustrations and work area plans are available to compare against.	5S operates a system that allows for controlled change and further improvement of 5S in the work areas. Scoring is kept on each of these 5's and history is present and visible to support future improvement.		
	XXV	Organization is now visible. Tool locations are known and allocated.	No self-discipline is necessary to ensure that all tools, equipment, gauges, and parts are put back in the same spot. No extra effort is needed to sustain 5S in the area.		
	XXVI	Evaluate the involvement of supervisors in 5S.	Supervisors are actively involved in the review process of 5S and are supporting improvement activities of the work areas.		
			Category Subtotal		
			Sustain Score: Subtotal divided by 4		

Total "Category Subtotals" divide by 26 average 5S score: TOTAL [ ]

Auto Body — 5S Audit Review Form

Date: _____   Evaluation Area: _____

5S Element	Number	Evaluation Criteria	Rank these items from 1 through 5: 5 being well done	Score (1-5)	Ideas / Suggestions / Comments
SORT	I	Are the aisles and walkways open and clear?	All items that are not necessary or unsafe have been removed from the area where people travel and work.		
	II	Is the work area free of any spills of fluids?	Consider whether there are any lubricants, water, oils or other materials that may be hazardous in the work area, on the floor, or under vehicles that are not necessary.		
	III	Is the work area free of unnecessary items and tools?	Are items that are not needed been removed from the work zone, i.e. tools, parts, cans, tags, extra items.		
	IV	Is the work area free of excess consumables/materials?	Evaluate against how many items are in the work area. Assess if the materials, parts, and supplies are currently needed for the repair area, staging area, point area, etc.		
	V	Is the production/ information board active and to what degree?	All jobs in each respective area of the shop are known and displayed. Announcements are current and in presentable shape. Arrangement is straight and placed under appropriate headings.		
	VI	Are the area's walls and dividers free of items not used in the shop?	Extra items are not on the walls, dividers, or hanging of signs that are not necessary.		

Category Subtotal _____

Sort Score: Subtotal divided by 6

5S Element	Number	Evaluation Criteria	Rank these items from 1 through 5: 5 being well done	Score (1-5)	Ideas / Suggestions / Comments
SET IN ORDER / STRAIGHTEN	VII	Evaluate any documentation storage.	Only documents to do the job are stored at the work area. Stock is limited and pre-staging is based on known lead-times throughput the repair shop. Documentation is understandable to outsiders		
	VIII	How are the shelves, desks, and work surfaces arranged?	All locations of items are labeled, marked, and it is known if they are missing.		
	IX	How are the tools and material used in operations stored?	No items are resting on or under automobiles nor tucked in corners. No items are resting on essential equipment, unknown in cupboards, or other places.		
	X	Evaluate temporary storage containers and staging locations and tidiness.	Parts, re-manufactured, components, and other items are stored in the appropriate place and orientated well for specific stage of the repair process. Items are secure and not causing any danger to the works.		
	XI	Assess orderliness of items on the shop's floor.	Minimal items are sitting directly on the floor and no materials are left around the vehicles. Items that need to be set on the floor are clearly marked and positioned in designated areas clearly outlined.		
	XII	Availability of tools for repair and teardown as well as measuring gauges.	Tools, components, measuring devices, and any fixtures need for teardown and repair are organized in a systematic way to ensure they are easily within reach and if not available are known where they are.		

Category Subtotal _____

Set in Order / Straighten Score: Subtotal divided by 6

5S Element	Number	Evaluation Criteria	Rank these items from 1 through 5: 5 being well done	Score (1-5)	Ideas / Suggestions / Comments
SHINE / SWEEP	XIII	The storage of gauges and tooling.	Arrangement and storage of all fixtures, tools, and gauges are kept in clean well organized and visual area for storage and no risk of damage or loss can occur.		
	XIV	Clear when equipment needs maintenance and when last maintained.	Machines are clearly marked, highlighted, and labeled. Compliance or check sheets are clean and displayed. Any maintenance is known scheduled; fluid levels, lubrication, and joints are accessible.		
	XV	In each department assess the cleanliness of the work area.	How dust free are the areas. Look under equipment, under vehicles, behind work benches, and tool chests to see if there is garbage and other unnecessary items.		
	XVI	Safety, are areas sectioned off and safe for workers?	Spray shields and physical guards are in active use to keep paint overspray and other sprays within the department. How much paint is getting on the floor. All critical areas are clearly marked to protect workers.		
	XVII	Assess status of equipment in the area. Cleanliness overall appearance.	Are machines, repair equipment, and other vehicles known to be on a maintenance schedule for cleaning and repair?		

Category Subtotal _____

Shine / Sweep Score: Subtotal divided by 5

5S Element	Number	Evaluation Criteria	Rank these items from 1 through 5: 5 being well done	Score (1-5)	Ideas / Suggestions / Comments
STANDARDIZE	XVIII	Is there visual color diagramming and color coding?	A clear and present color coding system is present in the work areas and across the shop. It's immediately clear that standards are being maintained and improved on.		
	XIX	Assess the access ways in case of emergency.	All emergency systems; fire vehicles, fire extinguishers, and emergency equipment free of obstruction and clear at all times. Access to electrical controls and fuses are known, marked, and free of any obstructions.		
	XX	The aisle ways are bright with light and clearly marked.	Walkways are clearly highlighted for direction, aisle access identified at any moment while in the work area. Transitional areas between the different departments and intersections are clearly marked.		
	XXI	General area has quantity limits for stored parts and are marked clearly.	Heights are marked, quantity of materials are known, and min vs. max is maintained. Shop carts are standardized to hold only parts for one vehicle. Large parts are clearly related to their respective cart.		
	XXII	Is there clear document control of information in the work zone?	All information and documentation is controlled, labeled, and revisions are up to date. There are no label-less binders or work orders in the area.		

Category Subtotal _____

Standardize Score: Subtotal divided by 5

5S Element	Number	Evaluation Criteria	Rank these items from 1 through 5: 5 being well done	Score (1-5)	Ideas / Suggestions / Comments
SUSTAIN	XXIII	The aisle ways are clean and maintenance is clear.	Aisles are never full of anything and are clear for passage. All vehicle parts are stored in work areas and only in designated storage areas next to aisles therefore allowing accessible movement in the area.		
	XXIV	Illustrations and work area plans are available to compare against.	5S operates a system that allows for controlled change and further improvement of 5S in the work areas. Scoring is kept on each of these 5's and history is present and visible to support future improvement.		
	XXV	Organization is now visible. Tool locations are known and allocated.	No self-discipline is necessary to ensure that all tools, equipment, gauges, and parts are put back in the same spot. No extra effort is needed to sustain 5S in the area.		
	XXVI	Evaluate the involvement of supervisors in 5S.	Supervisors are actively involved in the review process of 5S and are supporting improvement activities of the work areas.		

Category Subtotal _____

Sustain Score: Subtotal divided by 4

Total "Category Subtotals" divide by 26 average 5S score: TOTAL [_____]

Auto Body — 5S Audit Review Form

Date: _____   Evaluation Area: _____

5S Element	Number	Evaluation Criteria	Rank these items from 1 through 5: 5 being well done	Score (1-5)	Ideas / Suggestions / Comments
SORT	I	Are the aisles and walkways open and clear?	All items that are not necessary or unsafe have been removed from the area where people travel and work.		
	II	Is the work area free of any spills of fluids?	Consider whether there are any lubricants, water, oils or other materials that may be hazardous in the work area, on the floor, or under vehicles that are not necessary.		
	III	Is the work area free of unnecessary items and tools?	Are items that are not needed been removed from the work zone, i.e. tools, parts, cans, tags, extra items.		
	IV	Is the work area free of excess consumables/materials?	Evaluate against how many items are in the work area. Assess if the materials, parts, and supplies are currently needed for the repair area, staging area, point area, etc.		
	V	Is the production/ information board active and to what degree?	All jobs in each respective area of the shop are known and displayed. Announcements are current and in presentable shape. Arrangement is straight and placed under appropriate headings.		
	VI	Are the area's walls and dividers free of items not used in the shop?	Extra items are not on the walls, dividers, or hanging of signs that are not necessary.		
			Category Subtotal	- - - - - -	
			Sort Score: Subtotal divided by 6		
SET IN ORDER / STRAIGHTEN	VII	Evaluate any documentation storage.	Only documents to do the job are stored at the work area. Stock is limited and pre-staging is based on known lead-times throughput of the repair shop. Documentation is understandable to outsiders.		
	VIII	How are the shelves, desks, and work surfaces arranged?	All locations of items are labeled, marked, and it is known if they are missing.		
	IX	How are the tools and material used in operations stored?	No items are resting on or under automobiles nor tucked in corners. No items are resting on essential equipment, unknown in cupboards, or other places.		
	X	Evaluate temporary storage containers and staging locations and tidiness.	Parts, re-manufactured, components, and other items are stored in the appropriate place and orientated well for specific stage of the repair process. Items are secure and not causing any danger to the works.		
	XI	Assess orderliness of items on the shop's floor.	Minimal items are sitting directly on the floor and no materials are left around the vehicles. Items that need to be set on the floor are clearly marked and positioned in designated areas clearly outlined.		
	XII	Availability of tools for repair and teardown as well as measuring gauges.	Tools, components, measuring devices, and any fixtures need for teardown and repair are organized in a systematic way to ensure they are easily within reach and if not available are known where they are.		
			Category Subtotal	- - - - - -	
			Set in Order / Straighten Score: Subtotal divided by 6		
SHINE / SWEEP	XIII	The storage of gauges and tooling.	Arrangement and storage of all fixtures, tools, and gauges are kept in clean well organized and visual area for storage and no risk of damage or loss can occur.		
	XIV	Clear when equipment needs maintenance and when last maintained.	Machines are clearly marked, highlighted, and labeled. Compliance or check sheets are clean and displayed. Any maintenance is known scheduled; fluid levels, lubrication, and joints are accessible.		
	XV	In each department assess the cleanliness of the work area.	How dust free are the areas. Look under equipment, under vehicles, behind work benches, and tool chests to see if there is garbage and other unnecessary items.		
	XVI	Safety, are areas sectioned off and safe for workers?	Spray shields and physical guards are in active use to keep paint overspray and other sprays within the department. How much paint is getting on the floor. All critical areas are clearly marked to protect workers.		
	XVII	Assess status of equipment in the area. Cleanliness overall appearance.	Are machines, repair equipment, and other vehicles known to be on a maintenance schedule for cleaning and repair?		
			Category Subtotal	- - - - - -	
			Shine / Sweep Score: Subtotal divided by 5		
STANDARDIZE	XVIII	Is there visual color diagramming and color coding?	A clear and present color coding system is present in the work areas and across the shop. It's immediately clear that standards are being maintained and improved on.		
	XIX	Assess the access ways in case of emergency.	All emergency systems; fire vehicles, fire extinguishers, and emergency equipment free of obstruction and clear at all times. Access to electrical controls and fuses are known, marked, and free of any obstructions.		
	XX	The aisle ways are bright with light and clearly marked.	Walkways are clearly highlighted for direction, aisle access identified at any moment while in the work area. Transitional areas between the different departments and intersections are clearly marked.		
	XXI	General area has quantity limits for stored parts and are marked clearly.	Heights are marked, quantity of materials are known, and min vs. max is maintained. Shop carts are standardized to hold only parts for one vehicle. Large parts are clearly related to their respective cart.		
	XXII	Is there clear document control of information in the work zone?	All information and documentation is controlled, labeled, and revisions are up to date. There are no label-less binders or work orders in the area.		
			Category Subtotal	- - - - - -	
			Standardize Score: Subtotal divided by 5		
SUSTAIN	XXIII	The aisle ways are clean and maintenance is clear.	Aisles are never full of anything and are clear for passage. All vehicle parts are stored in work areas and only in designated storage areas next to aisles therefore allowing accessible movement in the area.		
	XXIV	Illustrations and work area plans are available to compare against.	5S operates a system that allows for controlled change and further improvement of 5S in the work areas. Scoring is kept on each of these 5's and history is present and visible to support future improvement.		
	XXV	Organization is now visible. Tool locations are known and allocated.	No self-discipline is necessary to ensure that all tools, equipment, gauges, and parts are put back in the same spot. No extra effort is needed to sustain 5S in the area.		
	XXVI	Evaluate the involvement of supervisors in 5S.	Supervisors are actively involved in the review process of 5S and are supporting improvement activities of the work areas.		
			Category Subtotal	- - - - - -	
			Sustain Score: Subtotal divided by 4		**Total "Category Subtotals" divide by 26 average 5S score: TOTAL** ☐

Auto Body — 5S Audit Review Form

Date: _____   Evaluation Area: _____

5S Element	Number	Evaluation Criteria	Rank these items from 1 through 5: 5 being well done	Score (1-5)	Ideas / Suggestions / Comments
SORT	I	Are the aisles and walkways open and clear?	All items that are not necessary or unsafe have been removed from the area where people travel and work.		
	II	Is the work area free of any spills of fluids?	Consider whether there are any lubricants, water, oils or other materials that may be hazardous in the work area, on the floor, or under vehicles that are not necessary.		
	III	Is the work area free of unnecessary items and tools?	Are items that are not needed been removed from the work zone, i.e. tools, parts, cans, tags, extra items.		
	IV	Is the work area free of excess consumables/materials?	Evaluate against how many items are in the work area. Assess if the materials, parts, and supplies are currently needed for the repair area, staging area, point area, etc.		
	V	Is the production/ information board active and to what degree?	All jobs in each respective area of the shop are known and displayed. Announcements are current and in presentable shape. Arrangement is straight and placed under appropriate headings.		
	VI	Are the area's walls and dividers free of items not used in the shop?	Extra items are not on the walls, dividers, or hanging of signs that are not necessary.		
		Category Subtotal		- - - - -	
		Sort Score: Subtotal divided by 6			
SET IN ORDER / STRAIGHTEN	VII	Evaluate any documentation storage.	Only documents to do the job are stored at the work area. Stock is limited and pre-staging is based on known lead-times throughput of the repair shop. Documentation is understandable to outsiders.		
	VIII	How are the shelves, desks, and work surfaces arranged?	All locations of items are labeled, marked, and it is known if they are missing.		
	IX	How are the tools and material used in operations stored?	No items are resting on or under automobiles nor tucked in corners. No items are resting on essential equipment, unknown in cupboards, or other places.		
	X	Evaluate temporary storage containers and staging locations and tidiness.	Parts, re-manufactured, components, and other items are stored in the appropriate place and orientated well for specific stage of the repair process. Items are secure and not causing any danger to the works.		
	XI	Assess orderliness of items on the shop's floor.	Minimal items are sitting directly on the floor and no materials are left around the vehicles. Items that need to be set on the floor are clearly marked and positioned in designated areas clearly outlined.		
	XII	Availability of tools for repair and teardown as well as measuring gauges.	Tools, components, measuring devices, and any fixtures need for teardown and repair are organized in a systematic way to ensure they are easily within reach and if not available are known where they are.		
		Category Subtotal		- - - - -	
		Set in Order / Straighten Score: Subtotal divided by 6			
SHINE / SWEEP	XIII	The storage of gauges and tooling.	Arrangement and storage of all fixtures, tools, and gauges are kept in clean well organized and visual area for storage and no risk of damage or loss can occur.		
	XIV	Clear when equipment needs maintenance and when last maintained.	Machines are clearly marked, highlighted, and labeled. Compliance or check sheets are clean and displayed. Any maintenance is known scheduled; fluid levels, lubrication, and joints are accessible.		
	XV	In each department assess the cleanliness of the work area.	How dust free are the areas. Look under equipment, under vehicles, behind work benches, and tool chests to see if there is garbage and other unnecessary items.		
	XVI	Safety, are areas sectioned off and safe for workers?	Spray shields and physical guards are in active use to keep paint overspray and other sprays within the department. How much paint is getting on the floor. All critical areas are clearly marked to protect workers.		
	XVII	Assess status of equipment in the area. Cleanliness overall appearance.	Are machines, repair equipment, and other vehicles known to be on a maintenance schedule for cleaning and repair?		
		Category Subtotal		- - - - -	
		Shine / Sweep Score: Subtotal divided by 5			
STANDARDIZE	XVIII	Is there visual color diagramming and color coding?	A clear and present color coding system is present in the work areas and across the shop. It's immediately clear that standards are being maintained and improved on.		
	XIX	Assess the access ways in case of emergency.	All emergency systems; fire vehicles, fire extinguishers, and emergency equipment free of obstruction and clear at all times. Access to electrical controls and fuses are known, marked, and free of any obstructions.		
	XX	The aisle ways are bright with light and clearly marked.	Walkways are clearly highlighted for direction, aisle access identified at any moment while in the work area. Transitional areas between the different departments and intersections are clearly marked.		
	XXI	General area has quantity limits for stored parts and are marked clearly.	Heights are marked, quantity of materials are known, and min vs. max is maintained. Shop carts are standardized to hold only parts for one vehicle. Large parts are clearly related to their respective cart.		
	XXII	Is there clear document control of information in the work zone?	All information and documentation is controlled, labeled, and revisions are up to date. There are no label-less binders or work orders in the area.		
		Category Subtotal		- - - - -	
		Standardize Score: Subtotal divided by 5			
SUSTAIN	XXIII	The aisle ways are clean and maintenance is clear.	Aisles are never full of anything and are clear for passage. All vehicle parts are stored in work areas and only in designated storage areas next to aisles therefore allowing accessible movement in the area.		
	XXIV	Illustrations and work area plans are available to compare against.	5S operates a system that allows for controlled change and further improvement of 5S in the work areas. Scoring is kept on each of these 5's and history is present and visible to support future improvement.		
	XXV	Organization is now visible. Tool locations are known and allocated.	No self-discipline is necessary to ensure that all tools, equipment, gauges, and parts are put back in the same spot. No extra effort is needed to sustain 5S in the area.		
	XXVI	Evaluate the involvement of supervisors in 5S.	Supervisors are actively involved in the review process of 5S and are supporting improvement activities of the work areas.		
		Category Subtotal		- - - - -	
		Sustain Score: Subtotal divided by 4			

Total "Category Subtotals" divide by 26 average 5S score: TOTAL [___]

Auto Body 5S Audit Review Form

Date: _____   Evaluation Area: _____

5S Element	Number	Evaluation Criteria	Rank these items from 1 through 5: 5 being well done	Score (1-5)	Ideas / Suggestions / Comments
SORT	I	Are the aisles and walkways open and clear?	All items that are not necessary or unsafe have been removed from the area where people travel and work.		
	II	Is the work area free of any spills of fluids?	Consider whether there are any lubricants, water, oils or other materials that may be hazardous in the work area, on the floor, or under vehicles that are not necessary.		
	III	Is the work area free of unnecessary items and tools?	Are items that are not needed been removed from the work zone, i.e. tools, parts, cans, tags, extra items.		
	IV	Is the work area free of excess consumables/materials?	Evaluate against how many items are in the work area. Assess if the materials, parts, and supplies are currently needed for the repair area, staging area, point area, etc.		
	V	Is the production/ information board active and to what degree?	All jobs in each respective area of the shop are known and displayed. Announcements are current and in presentable shape. Arrangement is straight and placed under appropriate headings.		
	VI	Are the area's walls and dividers free of items not used in the shop?	Extra items are not on the walls, dividers, or hanging of signs that are not necessary.		
			Category Subtotal		
			Sort Score: Subtotal divided by 6		
SET IN ORDER / STRAIGHTEN	VII	Evaluate any documentation storage	Only documents to do the job are stored at the work area. Stock is limited and pre-staging is based on known lead-times throughput of the repair shop. Documentation is understandable to outsiders.		
	VIII	How are the shelves, desks, and work surfaces arranged?	All locations of items are labeled, marked, and it is known if they are missing.		
	IX	How are the tools and material used in operations stored?	No items are resting on or under automobiles nor tucked in corners. No items are resting on essential equipment, unknown in cupboards, or other places.		
	X	Evaluate temporary storage containers and staging locations and tidiness.	Parts, re-manufactured, components, and other items are stored in the appropriate place and orientated well for specific stage of the repair process. Items are secure and not causing any danger to the works.		
	XI	Assess orderliness of items on the shop's floor.	Minimal items are sitting directly on the floor and no materials are left around the vehicles. Items that need to be set on the floor are clearly marked and positioned in designated areas clearly outlined.		
	XII	Availability of tools for repair and teardown as well as measuring gauges.	Tools, components, measuring devices, and any fixtures need for teardown and repair are organized in a systematic way to ensure they are easily within reach and if not available are known where they are.		
			Category Subtotal		
			Set in Order / Straighten Score: Subtotal divided by 6		
SHINE / SWEEP	XIII	The storage of gauges and tooling.	Arrangement and storage of all fixtures, tools, and gauges are kept in clean well organized and visual area for storage and no risk of damage or loss can occur.		
	XIV	Clear when equipment needs maintenance and when last maintained.	Machines are clearly marked, highlighted, and labeled. Compliance or check sheets are clean and displayed. Any maintenance is known scheduled; fluid levels, lubrication, and joints are accessible.		
	XV	In each department assess the cleanliness of the work area.	How dust free are the areas. Look under equipment, under vehicles, behind work benches, and tool chests to see if there is garbage and other unnecessary items.		
	XVI	Safety, are areas sectioned off and safe for workers?	Spray shields and physical guards are in active use to keep paint overspray and other sprays within the department. How much paint is getting on the floor. All critical areas are clearly marked to protect workers.		
	XVII	Assess status of equipment in the area. Cleanliness overall appearance.	Are machines, repair equipment, and other vehicles known to be on a maintenance schedule for cleaning and repair?		
			Category Subtotal		
			Shine / Sweep Score: Subtotal divided by 5		
STANDARDIZE	XVIII	Is there visual color diagramming and color coding?	A clear and present color coding system is present in the work areas and across the shop. It's immediately clear that standards are being maintained and improved on.		
	XIX	Assess the access ways in case of emergency.	All emergency systems; fire vehicles, fire extinguishers, and emergency equipment free of obstruction and clear at all times. Access to electrical controls and fuses are known, marked, and free of any obstructions.		
	XX	The aisle ways are bright with light and clearly marked.	Walkways are clearly highlighted for direction, aisle access identified at any moment while in the work area. Transitional areas between the different departments and intersections are clearly marked.		
	XXI	General area has quantity limits for stored parts and are marked clearly.	Heights are marked, quantity of materials are known, and min vs. max is maintained. Shop carts are standardized to hold only parts for one vehicle. Large parts are clearly related to their respective cart.		
	XXII	Is there clear document control of information in the work zone?	All information and documentation is controlled, labeled, and revisions are up to date. There are no label-less binders or work orders in the area.		
			Category Subtotal		
			Standardize Score: Subtotal divided by 5		
SUSTAIN	XXIII	The aisle ways are clean and maintenance is clear.	Aisles are never full of anything and are clear for passage. All vehicle parts are stored in work areas and only in designated storage areas next to aisles therefore allowing accessible movement in the area.		
	XXIV	Illustrations and work area plans are available to compare against.	5S operates a system that allows for controlled change and further improvement of 5S in the work areas. Scoring is kept on each of these 5's and history is present and visible to support future improvement.		
	XXV	Organization is now visible. Tool locations are known and allocated.	No self-discipline is necessary to ensure that all tools, equipment, gauges, and parts are put back in the same spot. No extra effort is needed to sustain 5S in the area.		
	XXVI	Evaluate the involvement of supervisors in 5S.	Supervisors are actively involved in the review process of 5S and are supporting improvement activities of the work areas.		
			Category Subtotal		
			Sustain Score: Subtotal divided by 4		

Total "Category Subtotals" divide by 26 average 5S score: TOTAL

Auto Body — 5S Audit Review Form

Date: _____   Evaluation Area: _____

5S Element	Number	Evaluation Criteria	Rank these items from 1 through 5: 5 being well done	Score (1-5)	Ideas / Suggestions / Comments
SORT	I	Are the aisles and walkways open and clear?	All items that are not necessary or unsafe have been removed from the area where people travel and work.		
	II	Is the work area free of any spills of fluids?	Consider whether there are any lubricants, water, oils or other materials that may be hazardous in the work area, on the floor, or under vehicles that are not necessary.		
	III	Is the work area free of unnecessary items and tools?	Are items that are not needed been removed from the work zone, i.e. tools, parts, cans, tags, extra items.		
	IV	Is the work area free of excess consumables/materials?	Evaluate against how many items are in the work area. Assess if the materials, parts, and supplies are currently needed for the repair area, staging area, point area, etc.		
	V	Is the production/ information board active and to what degree?	All jobs in each respective area of the shop are known and displayed. Announcements are current and in presentable shape. Arrangement is straight and placed under appropriate headings.		
	VI	Are the area's walls and dividers free of items not used in the shop?	Extra items are not on the walls, dividers, or hanging of signs that are not necessary.		
			Category Subtotal		
			Sort Score: Subtotal divided by 6		
SET IN ORDER / STRAIGHTEN	VII	Evaluate any documentation storage	Only documents to do the job are stored at the work area. Stock is limited and pre-staging is based on known lead-times throughput of the repair shop. Documentation is understandable to outsiders.		
	VIII	How are the shelves, desks, and work surfaces arranged?	All locations of items are labeled, marked, and it is known if they are missing.		
	IX	How are the tools and material used in operations stored?	No items are resting on or under automobiles nor tucked in corners. No items are resting on essential equipment, unknown in cupboards, or other places.		
	X	Evaluate temporary storage containers and staging locations and tidiness.	Parts, re-manufactured, components, and other items are stored in the appropriate place and orientated well for specific stage of the repair process. Items are secure and not causing any danger to the works.		
	XI	Assess orderliness of items on the shop's floor.	Minimal items are sitting directly on the floor and no materials are left around the vehicles. Items that need to be set on the floor are clearly marked and positioned in designated areas clearly outlined.		
	XII	Availability of tools for repair and teardown as well as measuring gauges.	Tools, components, measuring devices, and any fixtures need for teardown and repair are organized in a systematic way to ensure they are easily within reach and if not available are known where they are.		
			Category Subtotal		
			Set in Order / Straighten Score: Subtotal divided by 6		
SHINE / SWEEP	XIII	The storage of gauges and tooling.	Arrangement and storage of all fixtures, tools, and gauges are kept in clean well organized and visual area for storage and no risk of damage or loss can occur.		
	XIV	Clear when equipment needs maintenance and when last maintained.	Machines are clearly marked, highlighted, and labeled. Compliance or check sheets are clean and displayed. Any maintenance is known scheduled; fluid levels, lubrication, and joints are accessible.		
	XV	In each department assess the cleanliness of the work area.	How dust free are the areas. Look under equipment, under vehicles, behind work benches, and tool chests to see if there is garbage and other unnecessary items.		
	XVI	Safety, are areas sectioned off and safe for workers?	Spray shields and physical guards are in active use to keep paint overspray and other sprays within the department. How much paint is getting on the floor. All critical areas are clearly marked to protect workers.		
	XVII	Assess status of equipment in the area. Cleanliness overall appearance.	Are machines, repair equipment, and other vehicles known to be on a maintenance schedule for cleaning and repair?		
			Category Subtotal		
			Shine / Sweep Score: Subtotal divided by 5		
STANDARDIZE	XVIII	Is there visual color diagramming and color coding?	A clear and present color coding system is present in the work areas and across the shop. It's immediately clear that standards are being maintained and improved on.		
	XIX	Assess the access ways in case of emergency.	All emergency systems; fire vehicles, fire extinguishers, and emergency equipment free of obstruction and clear at all times. Access to electrical controls and fuses are known, marked, and free of any obstructions.		
	XX	The aisle ways are bright with light and clearly marked.	Walkways are clearly highlighted for direction, aisle access identified at any moment while in the work area. Transitional areas between the different departments and intersections are clearly marked.		
	XXI	General area has quantity limits for stored parts and are marked clearly.	Heights are marked, quantity of materials are known, and min vs. max is maintained. Shop carts are standardized to hold only parts for one vehicle. Large parts are clearly related to their respective cart.		
	XXII	Is there clear document control of information in the work zone?	All information and documentation is controlled, labeled, and revisions are up to date. There are no label-less binders or work orders in the area.		
			Category Subtotal		
			Standardize Score: Subtotal divided by 5		
SUSTAIN	XXIII	The aisle ways are clean and maintenance is clear.	Aisles are never full of anything and are clear for passage. All vehicle parts are stored in work areas and only in designated storage areas next to aisles therefore allowing accessible movement in the area.		
	XXIV	Illustrations and work area plans are available to compare against.	5S operates a system that allows for controlled change and further improvement of 5S in the work areas. Scoring is kept on each of these 5's and history is present and visible to support future improvement.		
	XXV	Organization is now visible. Tool locations are known and allocated.	No self-discipline is necessary to ensure that all tools, equipment, gauges, and parts are put back in the same spot. No extra effort is needed to sustain 5S in the area.		
	XXVI	Evaluate the involvement of supervisors in 5S.	Supervisors are actively involved in the review process of 5S and are supporting improvement activities of the work areas.		
			Category Subtotal		
			Sustain Score: Subtotal divided by 4		

Total "Category Subtotals" divide by 26 average 5S score: TOTAL

Auto Body 5S Audit Review Form

Date: _____   Evaluation Area: _____

5S Element	Number	Evaluation Criteria	Rank these items from 1 through 5: 5 being well done	Score (1-5)	Ideas / Suggestions / Comments
SORT	I	Are the aisles and walkways open and clear?	All items that are not necessary or unsafe have been removed from the area where people travel and work.		
	II	Is the work area free of any spills of fluids?	Consider whether there are any lubricants, water, oils or other materials that may be hazardous in the work area, on the floor, or under vehicles that are not necessary.		
	III	Is the work area free of unnecessary items and tools?	Are items that are not needed been removed from the work zone, i.e. tools, parts, cans, tags, extra items.		
	IV	Is the work area free of excess consumables/materials?	Evaluate against how many items are in the work area. Assess if the materials, parts, and supplies are currently needed for the repair area, staging area, point area, etc.		
	V	Is the production/ information board active and to what degree?	All jobs in each respective area of the shop are known and displayed. Announcements are current and in presentable shape. Arrangement is straight and placed under appropriate headings.		
	VI	Are the area's walls and dividers free of items not used in the shop?	Extra items are not on the walls, dividers, or hanging of signs that are not necessary.		
		Category Subtotal			
		Sort Score: Subtotal divided by 6			
SET IN ORDER / STRAIGHTEN	VII	Evaluate any documentation storage.	Only documents to do the job are stored at the work area. Stock is limited and pre-staging is based on known load times throughout of the repair shop. Documentation is understandable to outsiders.		
	VIII	How are the shelves, desks, and work surfaces arranged?	All locations of items are labeled, marked, and it is known if they are missing.		
	IX	How are the tools and material used in operations stored?	No items are resting on or under automobiles nor tucked in corners. No items are resting on essential equipment, unknown in cupboards, or other places.		
	X	Evaluate temporary storage containers and staging locations and tidiness.	Parts, re-manufactured, components, and other items are stored in the appropriate place and orientated well for specific stage of the repair process. Items are secure and not causing any danger to the works.		
	XI	Assess orderliness of items on the shop's floor.	Minimal items are sitting directly on the floor and no materials are left around the vehicles. Items that need to be set on the floor are clearly marked and positioned in designated areas clearly outlined.		
	XII	Availability of tools for repair and teardown as well as measuring gauges.	Tools, components, measuring devices, and any fixtures need for teardown and repair are organized in a systematic way to ensure they are easily within reach and if not available are known where they are.		
		Category Subtotal			
		Set in Order / Straighten Score: Subtotal divided by 6			
SHINE / SWEEP	XIII	The storage of gauges and tooling.	Arrangement and storage of all fixtures, tools, and gauges are kept in clean well organized and visual area for storage and no risk of damage or loss can occur.		
	XIV	Clear when equipment needs maintenance and when last maintained.	Machines are clearly marked, highlighted, and labeled. Compliance or check sheets are clean and displayed. Any maintenance is known scheduled; fluid levels, lubrication, and joints are accessible.		
	XV	In each department assess the cleanliness of the work area.	How dust free are the areas. Look under equipment, under vehicles, behind work benches, and tool chests to see if there is garbage and other unnecessary items.		
	XVI	Safety, are areas sectioned off and safe for workers?	Spray shields and physical guards are in active use to keep paint overspray and other sprays within the department. How much paint is getting on the floor. All critical areas are clearly marked to protect workers.		
	XVII	Assess status of equipment in the area. Cleanliness overall appearance.	Are machines, repair equipment, and other vehicles known to be on a maintenance schedule for cleaning and repair?		
		Category Subtotal			
		Shine / Sweep Score: Subtotal divided by 5			
STANDARDIZE	XVIII	Is there visual color diagramming and color coding?	A clear and present color coding system is present in the work areas and across the shop. It's immediately clear that standards are being maintained and improved on.		
	XIX	Assess the access ways in case of emergency.	All emergency systems; fire vehicles, fire extinguishers, and emergency equipment free of obstruction and clear at all times. Access to electrical controls and fuses are known, marked, and free of any obstructions.		
	XX	The aisle ways are bright with light and clearly marked.	Walkways are clearly highlighted for direction, aisle access identified at any moment while in the work area. Transitional areas between the different departments and intersections are clearly marked.		
	XXI	General area has quantity limits for stored parts and are marked clearly.	Heights are marked, quantity of materials are known, and min vs. max is maintained. Shop carts are standardized to hold only parts for one vehicle. Large parts are clearly related to their respective cart.		
	XXII	Is there clear document control of information in the work zone?	All information and documentation is controlled, labeled, and revisions are up to date. There are no label-less binders or work orders in the area.		
		Category Subtotal			
		Standardize Score: Subtotal divided by 5			
SUSTAIN	XXIII	The aisle ways are clean and maintenance is clear.	Aisles are never full of anything and are clear for passage. All vehicle parts are stored in work areas and only in designated storage areas next to aisles therefore allowing accessible movement in the area.		
	XXIV	Illustrations and work area plans are available to compare against.	5S operates a system that allows for controlled change and further improvement of 5S in the work areas. Scoring is kept on each of these 5's and history is present and visible to support future improvement.		
	XXV	Organization is now visible. Tool locations are known and allocated.	No self-discipline is necessary to ensure that all tools, equipment, gauges, and parts are put back in the same spot. No extra effort is needed to sustain 5S in the area.		
	XXVI	Evaluate the involvement of supervisors in 5S.	Supervisors are actively involved in the review process of 5S and are supporting improvement activities of the work areas.		
		Category Subtotal			
		Sustain Score: Subtotal divided by 4		Total "Category Subtotals" divide by 26 average 5S score: TOTAL

Auto Body — 5S Audit Review Form

Date: _____   Evaluation Area: _____

5S Element	Number	Evaluation Criteria	Rank these items from 1 through 5: 5 being well done	Score (1-5)	Ideas / Suggestions / Comments
SORT	I	Are the aisles and walkways open and clear?	All items that are not necessary or unsafe have been removed from the area where people travel and work.		
	II	Is the work area free of any spills of fluids?	Consider whether there are any lubricants, water, oils or other materials that may be hazardous in the work area, on the floor, or under vehicles that are not necessary.		
	III	Is the work area free of unnecessary items and tools?	Are items that are not needed been removed from the work zone, i.e. tools, parts, cans, tags, extra items.		
	IV	Is the work area free of excess consumables/materials?	Evaluate against how many items are in the work area. Assess if the materials, parts, and supplies are currently needed for the repair area, staging area, point area, etc.		
	V	Is the production/ information board active and to what degree?	All jobs in each respective area of the shop are known and displayed. Announcements are current and in presentable shape. Arrangement is straight and placed under appropriate headings.		
	VI	Are the area's walls and dividers free of items not used in the shop?	Extra items are not on the walls, dividers, or hanging of signs that are not necessary.		
			Category Subtotal		
			Sort Score: Subtotal divided by 6		
SET IN ORDER / STRAIGHTEN	VII	Evaluate any documentation storage.	Only documents to do the job are stored at the work area. Stock is limited and pre-staging is based on known lead-times throughput of the repair shop. Documentation is understandable to outsiders.		
	VIII	How are the shelves, desks, and work surfaces arranged?	All locations of items are labeled, marked, and it is known if they are missing.		
	IX	How are the tools and material used in operations stored?	No items are resting on or under automobiles nor tucked in corners. No items are resting on essential equipment, unknown in cupboards, or other places.		
	X	Evaluate temporary storage containers and staging locations and tidiness.	Parts, re-manufactured, components, and other items are stored in the appropriate place and orientated well for specific stage of the repair process. Items are secure and not causing any danger to the works.		
	XI	Assess orderliness of items on the shop's floor.	Minimal items are sitting directly on the floor and no materials are left around the vehicles. Items that need to be set on the floor are clearly marked and positioned in designated areas clearly outlined.		
	XII	Availability of tools for repair and teardown as well as measuring gauges.	Tools, components, measuring devices, and any fixtures need for teardown and repair are organized in a systematic way to ensure they are easily within reach and if not available are known where they are.		
			Category Subtotal		
			Set in Order / Straighten Score: Subtotal divided by 6		
SHINE / SWEEP	XIII	The storage of gauges and tooling.	Arrangement and storage of all fixtures, tools, and gauges are kept in clean well organized and visual area for storage and no risk of damage or loss can occur.		
	XIV	Clear when equipment needs maintenance and when last maintained.	Machines are clearly marked, highlighted, and labeled. Compliance or check sheets are clean and displayed. Any maintenance is known scheduled; fluid levels, lubrication, and joints are accessible.		
	XV	In each department assess the cleanliness of the work area.	How dust free are the areas. Look under equipment, under vehicles, behind work benches, and tool chests to see if there is garbage and other unnecessary items.		
	XVI	Safety, are areas sectioned off and safe for workers?	Spray shields and physical guards are in active use to keep paint overspray and other sprays within the department. How much paint is getting on the floor. All critical areas are clearly marked to protect workers.		
	XVII	Assess status of equipment in the area. Cleanliness overall appearance.	Are machines, repair equipment, and other vehicles known to be on a maintenance schedule for cleaning and repair?		
			Category Subtotal		
			Shine / Sweep Score: Subtotal divided by 5		
STANDARDIZE	XVIII	Is there visual color diagramming and color coding?	A clear and present color coding system is present in the work areas and across the shop. It's immediately clear that standards are being maintained and improved on.		
	XIX	Assess the access ways in case of emergency.	All emergency systems; fire vehicles, fire extinguishers, and emergency equipment free of obstruction and clear at all times. Access to electrical controls and fuses are known, marked, and free of any obstructions.		
	XX	The aisle ways are bright with light and clearly marked.	Walkways are clearly highlighted for direction, aisle access identified at any moment while in the work area. Transitional areas between the different departments and intersections are clearly marked.		
	XXI	General area has quantity limits for stored parts and are marked clearly.	Heights are marked, quantity of materials are known, and min vs. max is maintained. Shop carts are standardized to hold only parts for one vehicle. Large parts are clearly related to their respective cart.		
	XXII	Is there clear document control of information in the work zone?	All information and documentation is controlled, labeled, and revisions are up to date. There are no label-less binders or work orders in the area.		
			Category Subtotal		
			Standardize Score: Subtotal divided by 5		
SUSTAIN	XXIII	The aisle ways are clean and maintenance is clear.	Aisles are never full of anything and are clear for passage. All vehicle parts are stored in work areas and only in designated storage areas next to aisles therefore allowing accessible movement in the area.		
	XXIV	Illustrations and work area plans are available to compare against.	5S operates a system that allows for controlled change and further improvement of 5S in the work areas. Scoring is kept on each of these 5's and history is present and visible to support future improvement.		
	XXV	Organization is now visible. Tool locations are known and allocated.	No self-discipline is necessary to ensure that all tools, equipment, gauges, and parts are put back in the same spot. No extra effort is needed to sustain 5S in the area.		
	XXVI	Evaluate the involvement of supervisors in 5S.	Supervisors are actively involved in the review process of 5S and are supporting improvement activities of the work areas.		
			Category Subtotal		
			Sustain Score: Subtotal divided by 4		

Total "Category Subtotals" divide by 26 average 5S score: TOTAL [ ]

Auto Body 5S Audit Review Form

Date: _____   Evaluation Area: _____

5S Element	Number	Evaluation Criteria	Rank these items from 1 through 5: 5 being well done	Score (1-5)	Ideas / Suggestions / Comments
SORT	I	Are the aisles and walkways open and clear?	All items that are not necessary or unsafe have been removed from the area where people travel and work.		
	II	Is the work area free of any spills of fluids?	Consider whether there are any lubricants, water, oils or other materials that may be hazardous in the work area, on the floor, or under vehicles that are not necessary.		
	III	Is the work area free of unnecessary items and tools?	Are items that are not needed been removed from the work zone, i.e. tools, parts, cans, tags, extra items.		
	IV	Is the work area free of excess consumables/materials?	Evaluate against how many items are in the work area. Assess if the materials, parts, and supplies are currently needed for the repair area, staging area, point area, etc.		
	V	Is the production/ information board active and to what degree?	All jobs in each respective area of the shop are known and displayed. Announcements are current and in presentable shape. Arrangement is straight and placed under appropriate headings.		
	VI	Are the area's walls and dividers free of items not used in the shop?	Extra items are not on the walls, dividers, or hanging of signs that are not necessary.		
			Category Subtotal		
			Sort Score: Subtotal divided by 6		
SET IN ORDER / STRAIGHTEN	VII	Evaluate any documentation storage.	Only documents to do the job are stored at the work area. Stock is limited and pre-staging is based on known lead-times throughput of the repair shop. Documentation is understandable to outsiders.		
	VIII	How are the shelves, desks, and work surfaces arranged?	All locations of items are labeled, marked, and it is known if they are missing.		
	IX	How are the tools and material used in operations stored?	No items are resting on or under automobiles nor tucked in corners. No items are resting on essential equipment, unknown in cupboards, or other places.		
	X	Evaluate temporary storage containers and staging locations and tidiness.	Parts, re-manufactured, components, and other items are stored in the appropriate place and orientated well for specific stage of the repair process. Items are secure and not causing any danger to the works.		
	XI	Assess orderliness of items on the shop's floor.	Minimal items are sitting directly on the floor and no materials are left around the vehicles. Items that need to be set on the floor are clearly marked and positioned in designated areas clearly outlined.		
	XII	Availability of tools for repair and teardown as well as measuring gauges.	Tools, components, measuring devices, and any fixtures need for teardown and repair are organized in a systematic way to ensure they are easily within reach and if not available are known where they are.		
			Category Subtotal		
			Set in Order / Straighten Score: Subtotal divided by 6		
SHINE / SWEEP	XIII	The storage of gauges and tooling.	Arrangement and storage of all fixtures, tools, and gauges are kept in clean well organized and visual area for storage and no risk of damage or loss can occur.		
	XIV	Clear when equipment needs maintenance and when last maintained.	Machines are clearly marked, highlighted, and labeled. Compliance or check sheets are clean and displayed. Any maintenance is known scheduled; fluid levels, lubrication, and joints are accessible.		
	XV	In each department assess the cleanliness of the work area.	How dust free are the areas. Look under equipment, under vehicles, behind work benches, and tool chests to see if there is garbage and other unnecessary items.		
	XVI	Safety, are areas sectioned off and safe for workers?	Spray shields and physical guards are in active use to keep paint overspray and other sprays within the department. How much paint is getting on the floor. All critical areas are clearly marked to protect workers.		
	XVII	Assess status of equipment in the area. Cleanliness overall appearance.	Are machines, repair equipment, and other vehicles known to be on a maintenance schedule for cleaning and repair?		
			Category Subtotal		
			Shine / Sweep Score: Subtotal divided by 5		
STANDARDIZE	XVIII	Is there visual color diagramming and color coding?	A clear and present color coding system is present in the work areas and across the shop. It's immediately clear that standards are being maintained and improved on.		
	XIX	Assess the access ways in case of emergency.	All emergency systems; fire vehicles, fire extinguishers, and emergency equipment free of obstruction and clear at all times. Access to electrical controls and fuses are known, marked, and free of any obstructions.		
	XX	The aisle ways are bright with light and clearly marked.	Walkways are clearly highlighted for direction, aisle access identified at any moment while in the work area. Transitional areas between the different departments and intersections are clearly marked.		
	XXI	General area has quantity limits for stored parts and are marked clearly.	Heights are marked, quantity of materials are known, and min vs. max is maintained. Shop carts are standardized to hold only parts for one vehicle. Large parts are clearly related to their respective cart.		
	XXII	Is there clear document control of information in the work zone?	All information and documentation is controlled, labeled, and revisions are up to date. There are no label-less binders or work orders in the area.		
			Category Subtotal		
			Standardize Score: Subtotal divided by 5		
SUSTAIN	XXIII	The aisle ways are clean and maintenance is clear.	Aisles are never full of anything and are clear for passage. All vehicle parts are stored in work areas and only in designated storage areas next to aisles therefore allowing accessible movement in the area.		
	XXIV	Illustrations and work area plans are available to compare against.	5S operates a system that allows for controlled change and further improvement of 5S in the work areas. Scoring is kept on each of these 5's and history is present and visible to support future improvement.		
	XXV	Organization is now visible. Tool locations are known and allocated.	No self-discipline is necessary to ensure that all tools, equipment, gauges, and parts are put back in the same spot. No extra effort is needed to sustain 5S in the area.		
	XXVI	Evaluate the involvement of supervisors in 5S.	Supervisors are actively involved in the review process of 5S and are supporting improvement activities of the work areas.		
			Category Subtotal		
			Sustain Score: Subtotal divided by 4		

Total "Category Subtotals" divide by 26 average 5S score: TOTAL

Auto Body — 5S Audit Review Form

Date: _____   Evaluation Area: _____

5S Element	Number	Evaluation Criteria	Rank these items from 1 through 5: 5 being well done	Score (1-5)	Ideas / Suggestions / Comments
SORT	I	Are the aisles and walkways open and clear?	All items that are not necessary or unsafe have been removed from the area where people travel and work.		
	II	Is the work area free of any spills of fluids?	Consider whether there are any lubricants, water, oils or other materials that may be hazardous in the work area, on the floor, or under vehicles that are not necessary.		
	III	Is the work area free of unnecessary items and tools?	Are items that are not needed been removed from the work zone, i.e. tools, parts, cans, tags, extra items.		
	IV	Is the work area free of excess consumables/materials?	Evaluate against how many items are in the work area. Assess if the materials, parts, and supplies are currently needed for the repair area, staging area, point area, etc.		
	V	Is the production/ information board active and to what degree?	All jobs in each respective area of the shop are known and displayed. Announcements are current and in presentable shape. Arrangement is straight and placed under appropriate headings.		
	VI	Are the area's walls and dividers free of items not used in the shop?	Extra items are not on the walls, dividers, or hanging of signs that are not necessary.		
			Category Subtotal		
			Sort Score: Subtotal divided by 6		
SET IN ORDER / STRAIGHTEN	VII	Evaluate any documentation storage.	Only documents to do the job are stored at the work area. Stock is limited and pre-staging is based on known lead-times throughput of the repair shop. Documentation is understandable to outsiders.		
	VIII	How are the shelves, desks, and work surfaces arranged?	All locations of items are labeled, marked, and it is known if they are missing.		
	IX	How are the tools and material used in operations stored?	No items are resting on or under automobiles nor tucked in corners. No items are resting on essential equipment, unknown in cupboards, or other places.		
	X	Evaluate temporary storage containers and staging locations and tidiness.	Parts, re-manufactured, components, and other items are stored in the appropriate place and orientated well for specific stage of the repair process. Items are secure and not causing any danger to the works.		
	XI	Assess orderliness of items on the shop's floor.	Minimal items are sitting directly on the floor and no materials are left around the vehicles. Items that need to be set on the floor are clearly marked and positioned in designated areas clearly outlined.		
	XII	Availability of tools for repair and teardown as well as measuring gauges.	Tools, components, measuring devices, and any fixtures need for teardown and repair are organized in a systematic way to ensure they are easily within reach and if not available are known where they are.		
			Category Subtotal		
			Set in Order / Straighten Score: Subtotal divided by 6		
SHINE / SWEEP	XIII	The storage of gauges and tooling.	Arrangement and storage of all fixtures, tools, and gauges are kept in clean well organized and visual area for storage and no risk of damage or loss can occur.		
	XIV	Clear when equipment needs maintenance and when last maintained.	Machines are clearly marked, highlighted, and labeled. Compliance or check sheets are clean and displayed. Any maintenance is known scheduled; fluid levels, lubrication, and joints are accessible.		
	XV	In each department assess the cleanliness of the work area.	How dust free are the areas. Look under equipment, under vehicles, behind work benches, and tool chests to see if there is garbage and other unnecessary items.		
	XVI	Safety, are areas sectioned off and safe for workers?	Spray shields and physical guards are in active use to keep paint overspray and other sprays within the department. How much paint is getting on the floor. All critical areas are clearly marked to protect workers.		
	XVII	Assess status of equipment in the area. Cleanliness overall appearance.	Are machines, repair equipment, and other vehicles known to be on a maintenance schedule for cleaning and repair?		
			Category Subtotal		
			Shine / Sweep Score: Subtotal divided by 5		
STANDARDIZE	XVIII	Is there visual color diagramming and color coding?	A clear and present color coding system is present in the work areas and across the shop. It's immediately clear that standards are being maintained and improved on.		
	XIX	Assess the access ways in case of emergency.	All emergency systems; fire vehicles, fire extinguishers, and emergency equipment free of obstruction and clear at all times. Access to electrical controls and fuses are known, marked, and free of any obstructions.		
	XX	The aisle ways are bright with light and clearly marked.	Walkways are clearly highlighted for direction, aisle access identified at any moment while in the work area. Transitional areas between the different departments and intersections are clearly marked.		
	XXI	General area has quantity limits for stored parts and are marked clearly.	Heights are marked, quantity of materials are known, and min vs. max is maintained. Shop carts are standardized to hold only parts for one vehicle. Large parts are clearly related to their respective cart.		
	XXII	Is there clear document control of information in the work zone?	All information and documentation is controlled, labeled, and revisions are up to date. There are no label-less binders or work orders in the area.		
			Category Subtotal		
			Standardize Score: Subtotal divided by 5		
SUSTAIN	XXIII	The aisle ways are clean and maintenance is clear.	Aisles are never full of anything and are clear for passage. All vehicle parts are stored in work areas and only in designated storage areas next to aisles therefore allowing accessible movement in the area.		
	XXIV	Illustrations and work area plans are available to compare against.	5S operates a system that allows for controlled change and further improvement of 5S in the work areas. Scoring is kept on each of these 5's and history is present and visible to support future improvement.		
	XXV	Organization is now visible. Tool locations are known and allocated.	No self-discipline is necessary to ensure that all tools, equipment, gauges, and parts are put back in the same spot. No extra effort is needed to sustain 5S in the area.		
	XXVI	Evaluate the involvement of supervisors in 5S.	Supervisors are actively involved in the review process of 5S and are supporting improvement activities of the work areas.		
			Category Subtotal		
			Sustain Score: Subtotal divided by 4		

Total "Category Subtotals" divide by 26 average 5S score: TOTAL [_____]

Auto Body — 5S Audit Review Form

Date: _____   Evaluation Area: _____

5S Element	Number	Evaluation Criteria	Rank these items from 1 through 5: 5 being well done	Score (1-5)	Ideas / Suggestions / Comments
SORT	I	Are the aisles and walkways open and clear?	All items that are not necessary or unsafe have been removed from the area where people travel and work.		
	II	Is the work area free of any spills of fluids?	Consider whether there are any lubricants, water, oils or other materials that may be hazardous in the work area, on the floor, or under vehicles that are not necessary.		
	III	Is the work area free of unnecessary items and tools?	Are items that are not needed been removed from the work zone, i.e. tools, parts, cans, tags, extra items.		
	IV	Is the work area free of excess consumables/materials?	Evaluate against how many items are in the work area. Assess if the materials, parts, and supplies are currently needed for the repair area, staging area, point area, etc.		
	V	Is the production/ information board active and to what degree?	All jobs in each respective area of the shop are known and displayed. Announcements are current and in presentable shape. Arrangement is straight and placed under appropriate headings.		
	VI	Are the area's walls and dividers free of items not used in the shop?	Extra items are not on the walls, dividers, or hanging of signs that are not necessary.		
			Category Subtotal		
			Sort Score: Subtotal divided by 6		
SET IN ORDER / STRAIGHTEN	VII	Evaluate any documentation storage.	Only documents to do the job are stored at the work area. Stock is limited and pre-staging is based on known lead-times throughput of the repair shop. Documentation is understandable to outsiders.		
	VIII	How are the shelves, desks, and work surfaces arranged?	All locations of items are labeled, marked, and it is known if they are missing.		
	IX	How are the tools and material used in operations stored?	No items are resting on or under automobiles nor tucked in corners. No items are resting on essential equipment, unknown in cupboards, or other places.		
	X	Evaluate temporary storage containers and staging locations and tidiness.	Parts, re-manufactured, components, and other items are stored in the appropriate place and orientated well for specific stage of the repair process. Items are secure and not causing any danger to the works.		
	XI	Assess orderliness of items on the shop's floor.	Minimal items are sitting directly on the floor and no materials are left around the vehicles. Items that need to be set on the floor are clearly marked and positioned in designated areas clearly outlined.		
	XII	Availability of tools for repair and teardown as well as measuring gauges.	Tools, components, measuring devices, and any fixtures need for teardown and repair are organized in a systematic way to ensure they are easily within reach and if not available are known where they are.		
			Category Subtotal		
			Set in Order / Straighten Score: Subtotal divided by 6		
SHINE / SWEEP	XIII	The storage of gauges and tooling.	Arrangement and storage of all fixtures, tools, and gauges are kept in clean well organized and visual area for storage and no risk of damage or loss can occur.		
	XIV	Clear when equipment needs maintenance and when last maintained.	Machines are clearly marked, highlighted, and labeled. Compliance or check sheets are clean and displayed. Any maintenance is known scheduled; fluid levels, lubrication, and joints are accessible.		
	XV	In each department assess the cleanliness of the work area.	How dust free are the areas. Look under equipment, under vehicles, behind work benches, and tool chests to see if there is garbage and other unnecessary items.		
	XVI	Safety, are areas sectioned off and safe for workers?	Spray shields and physical guards are in active use to keep paint overspray and other sprays within the department. How much paint is getting on the floor. All critical areas are clearly marked to protect workers.		
	XVII	Assess status of equipment in the area. Cleanliness overall appearance.	Are machines, repair equipment, and other vehicles known to be on a maintenance schedule for cleaning and repair?		
			Category Subtotal		
			Shine / Sweep Score: Subtotal divided by 5		
STANDARDIZE	XVIII	Is there visual color diagramming and color coding?	A clear and present color coding system is present in the work areas and across the shop. It's immediately clear that standards are being maintained and improved on.		
	XIX	Assess the access ways in case of emergency.	All emergency systems; fire vehicles, fire extinguishers, and emergency equipment free of obstruction and clear at all times. Access to electrical controls and fuses are known, marked, and free of any obstructions.		
	XX	The aisle ways are bright with light and clearly marked.	Walkways are clearly highlighted for direction, aisle access identified at any moment while in the work area. Transitional areas between the different departments and intersections are clearly marked.		
	XXI	General area has quantity limits for stored parts and are marked clearly.	Heights are marked, quantity of materials are known, and min vs. max is maintained. Shop carts are standardized to hold only parts for one vehicle. Large parts are clearly related to their respective cart.		
	XXII	Is there clear document control of information in the work zone?	All information and documentation is controlled, labeled, and revisions are up to date. There are no label-less binders or work orders in the area.		
			Category Subtotal		
			Standardize Score: Subtotal divided by 5		
SUSTAIN	XXIII	The aisle ways are clean and maintenance is clear.	Aisles are never full of anything and are clear for passage. All vehicle parts are stored in work areas and only in designated storage areas next to aisles therefore allowing accessible movement in the area.		
	XXIV	Illustrations and work area plans are available to compare against.	5S operates a system that allows for controlled change and further improvement of 5S in the work areas. Scoring is kept on each of these 5's and history is present and visible to support future improvement.		
	XXV	Organization is now visible. Tool locations are known and allocated.	No self-discipline is necessary to ensure that all tools, equipment, gauges, and parts are put back in the same spot. No extra effort is needed to sustain 5S in the area.		
	XXVI	Evaluate the involvement of supervisors in 5S.	Supervisors are actively involved in the review process of 5S and are supporting improvement activities of the work areas.		
			Category Subtotal		
			Sustain Score: Subtotal divided by 4		

Total "Category Subtotals" divide by 26 average 5S score: TOTAL

Auto Body — 5S Audit Review Form

Date: _____   Evaluation Area: _____

5S Element	Number	Evaluation Criteria	Rank these items from 1 through 5: 5 being well done	Score (1-5)	Ideas / Suggestions / Comments
SORT	I	Are the aisles and walkways open and clear?	All items that are not necessary or unsafe have been removed from the area where people travel and work.		
	II	Is the work area free of any spills of fluids?	Consider whether there are any lubricants, water, oils or other materials that may be hazardous in the work area, on the floor, or under vehicles that are not necessary.		
	III	Is the work area free of unnecessary items and tools?	Are items that are not needed been removed from the work zone, i.e. tools, parts, cans, tags, extra items.		
	IV	Is the work area free of excess consumables/materials?	Evaluate against how many items are in the work area. Assess if the materials, parts, and supplies are currently needed for the repair area, staging area, point area, etc.		
	V	Is the production/ information board active and to what degree?	All jobs in each respective area of the shop are known and displayed. Announcements are current and in presentable shape. Arrangement is straight and placed under appropriate headings.		
	VI	Are the area's walls and dividers free of items not used in the shop?	Extra items are not on the walls, dividers, or hanging of signs that are not necessary.		

Category Subtotal ┄┄┄┄

Sort Score: Subtotal divided by 6

5S Element	Number	Evaluation Criteria	Rank these items from 1 through 5: 5 being well done	Score (1-5)	Ideas / Suggestions / Comments
SET IN ORDER / STRAIGHTEN	VII	Evaluate any documentation storage.	Only documents to do the job are stored at the work area. Stock is limited and pre-staging is based on known lead-times throughput of the repair shop. Documentation is understandable to outsiders.		
	VIII	How are the shelves, desks, and work surfaces arranged?	All locations of items are labeled, marked, and it is known if they are missing.		
	IX	How are the tools and material used in operations stored?	No items are resting on or under automobiles nor tucked in corners. No items are resting on essential equipment, unknown in cupboards, or other places.		
	X	Evaluate temporary storage containers and staging locations and tidiness.	Parts, re-manufactured, components, and other items are stored in the appropriate place and orientated well for specific stage of the repair process. Items are secure and not causing any danger to the works.		
	XI	Assess orderliness of items on the shop's floor.	Minimal items are sitting directly on the floor and no materials are left around the vehicles. Items that need to be set on the floor are clearly marked and positioned in designated areas clearly outlined.		
	XII	Availability of tools for repair and teardown as well as measuring gauges.	Tools, components, measuring devices, and any fixtures need for teardown and repair are organized in a systematic way to ensure they are easily within reach and if not available are known where they are.		

Category Subtotal ┄┄┄┄

Set in Order / Straighten Score: Subtotal divided by 6

5S Element	Number	Evaluation Criteria	Rank these items from 1 through 5: 5 being well done	Score (1-5)	Ideas / Suggestions / Comments
SHINE / SWEEP	XIII	The storage of gauges and tooling.	Arrangement and storage of all fixtures, tools, and gauges are kept in clean well organized and visual area for storage and no risk of damage or loss can occur.		
	XIV	Clear when equipment needs maintenance and when last maintained.	Machines are clearly marked, highlighted, and labeled. Compliance or check sheets are clean and displayed. Any maintenance is known scheduled; fluid levels, lubrication, and joints are accessible.		
	XV	In each department assess the cleanliness of the work area.	How dust free are the areas. Look under equipment, under vehicles, behind work benches, and tool chests to see if there is garbage and other unnecessary items.		
	XVI	Safety, are areas sectioned off and safe for workers?	Spray shields and physical guards are in active use to keep paint overspray and other sprays within the department. How much paint is getting on the floor. All critical areas are clearly marked to protect workers.		
	XVII	Assess status of equipment in the area. Cleanliness overall appearance.	Are machines, repair equipment, and other vehicles known to be on a maintenance schedule for cleaning and repair?		

Category Subtotal ┄┄┄┄

Shine / Sweep Score: Subtotal divided by 5

5S Element	Number	Evaluation Criteria	Rank these items from 1 through 5: 5 being well done	Score (1-5)	Ideas / Suggestions / Comments
STANDARDIZE	XVIII	Is there visual color diagramming and color coding?	A clear and present color coding system is present in the work areas and across the shop. It's immediately clear that standards are being maintained and improved on.		
	XIX	Assess the access ways in case of emergency.	All emergency systems; fire vehicles, fire extinguishers, and emergency equipment free of obstruction and clear at all times. Access to electrical controls and fuses are known, marked, and free of any obstructions.		
	XX	The aisle ways are bright with light and clearly marked.	Walkways are clearly highlighted for direction, aisle access identified at any moment while in the work area. Transitional areas between the different departments and intersections are clearly marked.		
	XXI	General area has quantity limits for stored parts and are marked clearly.	Heights are marked, quantity of materials are known, and min vs. max is maintained. Shop carts are standardized to hold only parts for one vehicle. Large parts are clearly related to their respective cart.		
	XXII	Is there clear document control of information in the work zone?	All information and documentation is controlled, labeled, and revisions are up to date. There are no label-less binders or work orders in the area.		

Category Subtotal ┄┄┄┄

Standardize Score: Subtotal divided by 5

5S Element	Number	Evaluation Criteria	Rank these items from 1 through 5: 5 being well done	Score (1-5)	Ideas / Suggestions / Comments
SUSTAIN	XXIII	The aisle ways are clean and maintenance is clear.	Aisles are never full of anything and are clear for passage. All vehicle parts are stored in work areas and only in designated storage areas next to aisles therefore allowing accessible movement in the area.		
	XXIV	Illustrations and work area plans are available to compare against.	5S operates a system that allows for controlled change and further improvement of 5S in the work areas. Scoring is kept on each of these 5's and history is present and visible to support future improvement.		
	XXV	Organization is now visible. Tool locations are known and allocated.	No self-discipline is necessary to ensure that all tools, equipment, gauges, and parts are put back in the same spot. No extra effort is needed to sustain 5S in the area.		
	XXVI	Evaluate the involvement of supervisors in 5S.	Supervisors are actively involved in the review process of 5S and are supporting improvement activities of the work areas.		

Category Subtotal ┄┄┄┄

Sustain Score: Subtotal divided by 4

Total "Category Subtotals" divide by 26 average 5S score: TOTAL [_____]

Auto Body — 5S Audit Review Form

Date: _____ Evaluation Area: _____

5S Element	Number	Evaluation Criteria	Rank these items from 1 through 5: 5 being well done	Score (1-5)	Ideas / Suggestions / Comments
SORT	I	Are the aisles and walkways open and clear?	All items that are not necessary or unsafe have been removed from the area where people travel and work.		
	II	Is the work area free of any spills of fluids?	Consider whether there are any lubricants, water, oils or other materials that may be hazardous in the work area, on the floor, or under vehicles that are not necessary.		
	III	Is the work area free of unnecessary items and tools?	Are items that are not needed been removed from the work zone, i.e. tools, parts, cans, tags, extra items.		
	IV	Is the work area free of excess consumables/materials?	Evaluate against how many items are in the work area. Assess if the materials, parts, and supplies are currently needed for the repair area, staging area, point area, etc.		
	V	Is the production/ information board active and to what degree?	All jobs in each respective area of the shop are known and displayed. Announcements are current and in presentable shape. Arrangement is straight and placed under appropriate headings.		
	VI	Are the area's walls and dividers free of items not used in the shop?	Extra items are not on the walls, dividers, or hanging of signs that are not necessary.		
		Category Subtotal			
		Sort Score: Subtotal divided by 6			
SET IN ORDER / STRAIGHTEN	VII	Evaluate any documentation storage.	Only documents to do the job are stored at the work area. Stock is limited and pre-staging is based on known lead-times throughput of the repair shop. Documentation is understandable to outsiders.		
	VIII	How are the shelves, desks, and work surfaces arranged?	All locations of items are labeled, marked, and it is known if they are missing.		
	IX	How are the tools and material used in operations stored?	No items are resting on or under automobiles nor tucked in corners. No items are resting on essential equipment, unknown in cupboards, or other places.		
	X	Evaluate temporary storage containers and staging locations and tidiness.	Parts, re-manufactured, components, and other items are stored in the appropriate place and orientated well for specific stage of the repair process. Items are secure and not causing any danger to the works.		
	XI	Assess orderliness of items on the shop's floor.	Minimal items are sitting directly on the floor and no materials are left around the vehicles. Items that need to be set on the floor are clearly marked and positioned in designated areas clearly outlined.		
	XII	Availability of tools for repair and teardown as well as measuring gauges.	Tools, components, measuring devices, and any fixtures need for teardown and repair are organized in a systematic way to ensure they are easily within reach and if not available are known where they are.		
		Category Subtotal			
		Set in Order / Straighten Score: Subtotal divided by 6			
SHINE / SWEEP	XIII	The storage of gauges and tooling.	Arrangement and storage of all fixtures, tools, and gauges are kept in clean well organized and visual area for storage and no risk of damage or loss can occur.		
	XIV	Clear when equipment needs maintenance and when last maintained.	Machines are clearly marked, highlighted, and labeled. Compliance or check sheets are clean and displayed. Any maintenance is known scheduled; fluid levels, lubrication, and joints are accessible.		
	XV	In each department assess the cleanliness of the work area.	How dust free are the areas. Look under equipment, under vehicles, behind work benches, and tool chests to see if there is garbage and other unnecessary items.		
	XVI	Safety, are areas sectioned off and safe for workers?	Spray shields and physical guards are in active use to keep paint overspray and other sprays within the department. How much paint is getting on the floor. All critical areas are clearly marked to protect workers.		
	XVII	Assess status of equipment in the area. Cleanliness overall appearance.	Are machines, repair equipment, and other vehicles known to be on a maintenance schedule for cleaning and repair?		
		Category Subtotal			
		Shine / Sweep Score: Subtotal divided by 5			
STANDARDIZE	XVIII	Is there visual color diagramming and color coding?	A clear and present color coding system is present in the work areas and across the shop. It's immediately clear that standards are being maintained and improved on.		
	XIX	Assess the access ways in case of emergency.	All emergency systems; fire vehicles, fire extinguishers, and emergency equipment free of obstruction and clear at all times. Access to electrical controls and fuses are known, marked, and free of any obstructions.		
	XX	The aisle ways are bright with light and clearly marked.	Walkways are clearly highlighted for direction, aisle access identified at any moment while in the work area. Transitional areas between the different departments and intersections are clearly marked.		
	XXI	General area has quantity limits for stored parts and are marked clearly.	Heights are marked, quantity of materials are known, and min vs. max is maintained. Shop carts are standardized to hold only parts for one vehicle. Large parts are clearly related to their respective cart.		
	XXII	Is there clear document control of information in the work zone?	All information and documentation is controlled, labeled, and revisions are up to date. There are no label-less binders or work orders in the area.		
		Category Subtotal			
		Standardize Score: Subtotal divided by 5			
SUSTAIN	XXIII	The aisle ways are clean and maintenance is clear.	Aisles are never full of anything and are clear for passage. All vehicle parts are stored in work areas and only in designated storage areas next to aisles therefore allowing accessible movement in the area.		
	XXIV	Illustrations and work area plans are available to compare against.	5S operates a system that allows for controlled change and further improvement of 5S in the work areas. Scoring is kept on each of these 5's and history is present and visible to support future improvement.		
	XXV	Organization is now visible. Tool locations are known and allocated.	No self-discipline is necessary to ensure that all tools, equipment, gauges, and parts are put back in the same spot. No extra effort is needed to sustain 5S in the area.		
	XXVI	Evaluate the involvement of supervisors in 5S.	Supervisors are actively involved in the review process of 5S and are supporting improvement activities of the work areas.		
		Category Subtotal			
		Sustain Score: Subtotal divided by 4			

Total "Category Subtotals" divide by 26 average 5S score: TOTAL [____]

Auto Body — 5S Audit Review Form

Date: _____   Evaluation Area: _____

5S Element	Number	Evaluation Criteria	Rank these items from 1 through 5: 5 being well done	Score (1-5)	Ideas / Suggestions / Comments
SORT	I	Are the aisles and walkways open and clear?	All items that are not necessary or unsafe have been removed from the area where people travel and work.		
	II	Is the work area free of any spills of fluids?	Consider whether there are any lubricants, water, oils or other materials that may be hazardous in the work area, on the floor, or under vehicles that are not necessary.		
	III	Is the work area free of unnecessary items and tools?	Are items that are not needed been removed from the work zone, i.e. tools, parts, cans, tags, extra items.		
	IV	Is the work area free of excess consumables/materials?	Evaluate against how many items are in the work area. Assess if the materials, parts, and supplies are currently needed for the repair area, staging area, point area, etc.		
	V	Is the production/ information board active and to what degree?	All jobs in each respective area of the shop are known and displayed. Announcements are current and in presentable shape. Arrangement is straight and placed under appropriate headings.		
	VI	Are the area's walls and dividers free of items not used in the shop?	Extra items are not on the walls, dividers, or hanging of signs that are not necessary.		
			Category Subtotal		
			Sort Score: Subtotal divided by 6		
SET IN ORDER / STRAIGHTEN	VII	Evaluate any documentation storage.	Only documents to do the job are stored at the work area. Stock is limited and pre-staging is based on known lead-times throughout the repair shop. Documentation is understandable to outsiders.		
	VIII	How are the shelves, desks, and work surfaces arranged?	All locations of items are labeled, marked, and it is known if they are missing.		
	IX	How are the tools and material used in operations stored?	No items are resting on or under automobiles nor tucked in corners. No items are resting on essential equipment, unknown in cupboards, or other places.		
	X	Evaluate temporary storage containers and staging locations and tidiness.	Parts, re-manufactured, components, and other items are stored in the appropriate place and orientated well for specific stage of the repair process. Items are secure and not causing any danger to the works.		
	XI	Assess orderliness of items on the shop's floor.	Minimal items are sitting directly on the floor and no materials are left around the vehicles. Items that need to be set on the floor are clearly marked and positioned in designated areas clearly outlined.		
	XII	Availability of tools for repair and teardown as well as measuring gauges.	Tools, components, measuring devices, and any fixtures need for teardown and repair are organized in a systematic way to ensure they are easily within reach and if not available are known where they are.		
			Category Subtotal		
			Set in Order / Straighten Score: Subtotal divided by 6		
SHINE / SWEEP	XIII	The storage of gauges and tooling.	Arrangement and storage of all fixtures, tools, and gauges are kept in clean well organized and visual area for storage and no risk of damage or loss can occur.		
	XIV	Clear when equipment needs maintenance and when last maintained.	Machines are clearly marked, highlighted, and labeled. Compliance or check sheets are clean and displayed. Any maintenance is known scheduled; fluid levels, lubrication, and joints are accessible.		
	XV	In each department assess the cleanliness of the work area.	How dust free are the areas. Look under equipment, under vehicles, behind work benches, and tool chests to see if there is garbage and other unnecessary items.		
	XVI	Safety, are areas sectioned off and safe for workers?	Spray shields and physical guards are in active use to keep paint overspray and other sprays within the department. How much paint is getting on the floor. All critical areas are clearly marked to protect workers.		
	XVII	Assess status of equipment in the area. Cleanliness overall appearance.	Are machines, repair equipment, and other vehicles known to be on a maintenance schedule for cleaning and repair?		
			Category Subtotal		
			Shine / Sweep Score: Subtotal divided by 5		
STANDARDIZE	XVIII	Is there visual color diagramming and color coding?	A clear and present color coding system is present in the work areas and across the shop. It's immediately clear that standards are being maintained and improved on.		
	XIX	Assess the access ways in case of emergency.	All emergency systems; fire vehicles, fire extinguishers, and emergency equipment free of obstruction and clear at all times. Access to electrical controls and fuses are known, marked, and free of any obstructions.		
	XX	The aisle ways are bright with light and clearly marked.	Walkways are clearly highlighted for direction, aisle access identified at any moment while in the work area. Transitional areas between the different departments and intersections are clearly marked.		
	XXI	General area has quantity limits for stored parts and are marked clearly.	Heights are marked, quantity of materials are known, and min vs. max is maintained. Shop carts are standardized to hold only parts for one vehicle. Large parts are clearly related to their respective cart.		
	XXII	Is there clear document control of information in the work zone?	All information and documentation is controlled, labeled, and revisions are up to date. There are no label-less binders or work orders in the area.		
			Category Subtotal		
			Standardize Score: Subtotal divided by 5		
SUSTAIN	XXIII	The aisle ways are clean and maintenance is clear.	Aisles are never full of anything and are clear for passage. All vehicle parts are stored in work areas and only in designated storage areas next to aisles therefore allowing accessible movement in the area.		
	XXIV	Illustrations and work area plans are available to compare against.	5S operates a system that allows for controlled change and further improvement of 5S in the work areas. Scoring is kept on each of these 5's and history is present and visible to support future improvement.		
	XXV	Organization is now visible. Tool locations are known and allocated.	No self-discipline is necessary to ensure that all tools, equipment, gauges, and parts are put back in the same spot. No extra effort is needed to sustain 5S in the area.		
	XXVI	Evaluate the involvement of supervisors in 5S.	Supervisors are actively involved in the review process of 5S and are supporting improvement activities of the work areas.		
			Category Subtotal		
			Sustain Score: Subtotal divided by 4		

Total "Category Subtotals" divide by 26 average 5S score: TOTAL ☐

Auto Body — 5S Audit Review Form

Date: _____   Evaluation Area: _____

5S Element	Number	Evaluation Criteria	Rank these items from 1 through 5: 5 being well done	Score (1-5)	Ideas / Suggestions / Comments
SORT	I	Are the aisles and walkways open and clear?	All items that are not necessary or unsafe have been removed from the area where people travel and work.		
	II	Is the work area free of any spills of fluids?	Consider whether there are any lubricants, water, oils or other materials that may be hazardous in the work area, on the floor, or under vehicles that are not necessary.		
	III	Is the work area free of unnecessary items and tools?	Are items that are not needed been removed from the work zone, i.e. tools, parts, cans, tags, extra items.		
	IV	Is the work area free of excess consumables/materials?	Evaluate against how many items are in the work area. Assess if the materials, parts, and supplies are currently needed for the repair area, staging area, point area, etc.		
	V	Is the production/ information board active and to what degree?	All jobs in each respective area of the shop are known and displayed. Announcements are current and in presentable shape. Arrangement is straight and placed under appropriate headings.		
	VI	Are the area's walls and dividers free of items not used in the shop?	Extra items are not on the walls, dividers, or hanging of signs that are not necessary.		
		Category Subtotal		-------	
		Sort Score: Subtotal divided by 6			
SET IN ORDER / STRAIGHTEN	VII	Evaluate any documentation storage.	Only documents to do the job are stored at the work area. Stock is limited and pre-staging is based on known lead-times throughput of the repair shop. Documentation is understandable to outsiders.		
	VIII	How are the shelves, desks, and work surfaces arranged?	All locations of items are labeled, marked, and it is known if they are missing.		
	IX	How are the tools and material used in operations stored?	No items are resting on or under automobiles nor tucked in corners. No items are resting on essential equipment, unknown in cupboards, or other places.		
	X	Evaluate temporary storage containers and staging locations and tidiness.	Parts, re-manufactured, components, and other items are stored in the appropriate place and orientated well for specific stage of the repair process. Items are secure and not causing any danger to the works.		
	XI	Assess orderliness of items on the shop's floor.	Minimal items are sitting directly on the floor and no materials are left around the vehicles. Items that need to be set on the floor are clearly marked and positioned in designated areas clearly outlined.		
	XII	Availability of tools for repair and teardown as well as measuring gauges.	Tools, components, measuring devices, and any fixtures need for teardown and repair are organized in a systematic way to ensure they are easily within reach and if not available are known where they are.		
		Category Subtotal		-------	
		Set in Order / Straighten Score: Subtotal divided by 6			
SHINE / SWEEP	XIII	The storage of gauges and tooling.	Arrangement and storage of all fixtures, tools, and gauges are kept in clean well organized and visual area for storage and no risk of damage or loss can occur.		
	XIV	Clear when equipment needs maintenance and when last maintained.	Machines are clearly marked, highlighted, and labeled. Compliance or check sheets are clean and displayed. Any maintenance is known scheduled; fluid levels, lubrication, and joints are accessible.		
	XV	In each department assess the cleanliness of the work area.	How dust free are the areas. Look under equipment, under vehicles, behind work benches, and tool chests to see if there is garbage and other unnecessary items.		
	XVI	Safety, are areas sectioned off and safe for workers?	Spray shields and physical guards are in active use to keep paint overspray and other sprays within the department. How much paint is getting on the floor. All critical areas are clearly marked to protect workers.		
	XVII	Assess status of equipment in the area. Cleanliness overall appearance.	Are machines, repair equipment, and other vehicles known to be on a maintenance schedule for cleaning and repair?		
		Category Subtotal		-------	
		Shine / Sweep Score: Subtotal divided by 5			
STANDARDIZE	XVIII	Is there visual color diagramming and color coding?	A clear and present color coding system is present in the work areas and across the shop. It's immediately clear that standards are being maintained and improved on.		
	XIX	Assess the access ways in case of emergency.	All emergency systems; fire vehicles, fire extinguishers, and emergency equipment free of obstruction and clear at all times. Access to electrical controls and fuses are known, marked, and free of any obstructions.		
	XX	The aisle ways are bright with light and clearly marked.	Walkways are clearly highlighted for direction, aisle access identified at any moment while in the work area. Transitional areas between the different departments and intersections are clearly marked.		
	XXI	General area has quantity limits for stored parts and are marked clearly.	Heights are marked, quantity of materials are known, and min vs. max is maintained. Shop carts are standardized to hold only parts for one vehicle. Large parts are clearly related to their respective cart.		
	XXII	Is there clear document control of information in the work zone?	All information and documentation is controlled, labeled, and revisions are up to date. There are no label-less binders or work orders in the area.		
		Category Subtotal		-------	
		Standardize Score: Subtotal divided by 5			
SUSTAIN	XXIII	The aisle ways are clean and maintenance is clear.	Aisles are never full of anything and are clear for passage. All vehicle parts are stored in work areas and only in designated storage areas next to aisles therefore allowing accessible movement in the area.		
	XXIV	Illustrations and work area plans are available to compare against.	5S operates a system that allows for controlled change and further improvement of 5S in the work areas. Scoring is kept on each of these 5's and history is present and visible to support future improvement.		
	XXV	Organization is now visible. Tool locations are known and allocated.	No self-discipline is necessary to ensure that all tools, equipment, gauges, and parts are put back in the same spot. No extra effort is needed to sustain 5S in the area.		
	XXVI	Evaluate the involvement of supervisors in 5S.	Supervisors are actively involved in the review process of 5S and are supporting improvement activities of the work areas.		
		Category Subtotal		-------	
		Sustain Score: Subtotal divided by 4			**Total "Category Subtotals" divide by 26 average 5S score: TOTAL** [_____]

Auto Body — 5S Audit Review Form

Date: _____ Evaluation Area: _____

5S Element	Number	Evaluation Criteria	Rank these items from 1 through 5: 5 being well done	Score (1-5)	Ideas / Suggestions / Comments
SORT	I	Are the aisles and walkways open and clear?	All items that are not necessary or unsafe have been removed from the area where people travel and work.		
	II	Is the work area free of any spills of fluids?	Consider whether there are any lubricants, water, oils or other materials that may be hazardous in the work area, on the floor, or under vehicles that are not necessary.		
	III	Is the work area free of unnecessary items and tools?	Are items that are not needed been removed from the work zone, i.e. tools, parts, cans, tags, extra items.		
	IV	Is the work area free of excess consumables/materials?	Evaluate against how many items are in the work area. Assess if the materials, parts, and supplies are currently needed for the repair area, staging area, point area, etc.		
	V	Is the production/ information board active and to what degree?	All jobs in each respective area of the shop are known and displayed. Announcements are current and in presentable shape. Arrangement is straight and placed under appropriate headings.		
	VI	Are the area's walls and dividers free of items not used in the shop?	Extra items are not on the walls, dividers, or hanging of signs that are not necessary.		
			Category Subtotal		
			Sort Score: Subtotal divided by 6		
SET IN ORDER / STRAIGHTEN	VII	Evaluate any documentation storage.	Only documents to do the job are stored at the work area. Stock is limited and pre-staging is based on known lead-times throughput of the repair shop. Documentation is understandable to outsiders.		
	VIII	How are the shelves, desks, and work surfaces arranged?	All locations of items are labeled, marked, and it is known if they are missing.		
	IX	How are the tools and material used in operations stored?	No items are resting on or under automobiles nor tucked in corners. No items are resting on essential equipment, unknown in cupboards, or other places.		
	X	Evaluate temporary storage containers and staging locations and tidiness.	Parts, re-manufactured, components, and other items are stored in the appropriate place and orientated well for specific stage of the repair process. Items are secure and not causing any danger to the works.		
	XI	Assess orderliness of items on the shop's floor.	Minimal items are sitting directly on the floor and no materials are left around the vehicles. Items that need to be set on the floor are clearly marked and positioned in designated areas clearly outlined.		
	XII	Availability of tools for repair and teardown as well as measuring gauges.	Tools, components, measuring devices, and any fixtures need for teardown and repair are organized in a systematic way to ensure they are easily within reach and if not available are known where they are.		
			Category Subtotal		
			Set in Order / Straighten Score: Subtotal divided by 6		
SHINE / SWEEP	XIII	The storage of gauges and tooling.	Arrangement and storage of all fixtures, tools, and gauges are kept in clean well organized and visual area for storage and no risk of damage or loss can occur.		
	XIV	Clear when equipment needs maintenance and when last maintained.	Machines are clearly marked, highlighted, and labeled. Compliance or check sheets are clean and displayed. Any maintenance is known scheduled; fluid levels, lubrication, and joints are accessible.		
	XV	In each department assess the cleanliness of the work area.	How dust free are the areas. Look under equipment, under vehicles, behind work benches, and tool chests to see if there is garbage and other unnecessary items.		
	XVI	Safety, are areas sectioned off and safe for workers?	Spray shields and physical guards are in active use to keep paint overspray and other sprays within the department. How much paint is getting on the floor. All critical areas are clearly marked to protect workers.		
	XVII	Assess status of equipment in the area. Cleanliness overall appearance.	Are machines, repair equipment, and other vehicles known to be on a maintenance schedule for cleaning and repair?		
			Category Subtotal		
			Shine / Sweep Score: Subtotal divided by 5		
STANDARDIZE	XVIII	Is there visual color diagramming and color coding?	A clear and present color coding system is present in the work areas and across the shop. It's immediately clear that standards are being maintained and improved on.		
	XIX	Assess the access ways in case of emergency.	All emergency systems; fire vehicles, fire extinguishers, and emergency equipment free of obstruction and clear at all times. Access to electrical controls and fuses are known, marked, and free of any obstructions.		
	XX	The aisle ways are bright with light and clearly marked.	Walkways are clearly highlighted for direction, aisle access identified at any moment while in the work area. Transitional areas between the different departments and intersections are clearly marked.		
	XXI	General area has quantity limits for stored parts and are marked clearly.	Heights are marked, quantity of materials are known, and min vs. max is maintained. Shop carts are standardized to hold only parts for one vehicle. Large parts are clearly related to their respective cart.		
	XXII	Is there clear document control of information in the work zone?	All information and documentation is controlled, labeled, and revisions are up to date. There are no label-less binders or work orders in the area.		
			Category Subtotal		
			Standardize Score: Subtotal divided by 5		
SUSTAIN	XXIII	The aisle ways are clean and maintenance is clear.	Aisles are never full of anything and are clear for passage. All vehicle parts are stored in work areas and only in designated storage areas next to aisles therefore allowing accessible movement in the area.		
	XXIV	Illustrations and work area plans are available to compare against.	5S operates a system that allows for controlled change and further improvement of 5S in the work areas. Scoring is kept on each of these 5's and history is present and visible to support future improvement.		
	XXV	Organization is now visible. Tool locations are known and allocated.	No self-discipline is necessary to ensure that all tools, equipment, gauges, and parts are put back in the same spot. No extra effort is needed to sustain 5S in the area.		
	XXVI	Evaluate the involvement of supervisors in 5S.	Supervisors are actively involved in the review process of 5S and are supporting improvement activities of the work areas.		
			Category Subtotal		
			Sustain Score: Subtotal divided by 4		**Total "Category Subtotals" divide by 26 average 5S score: TOTAL**

Auto Body — 5S Audit Review Form

Date: _____   Evaluation Area: _____

5S Element	Number	Evaluation Criteria	Rank these items from 1 through 5: 5 being well done	Score (1-5)	Ideas / Suggestions / Comments
SORT	I	Are the aisles and walkways open and clear?	All items that are not necessary or unsafe have been removed from the area where people travel and work.		
	II	Is the work area free of any spills of fluids?	Consider whether there are any lubricants, water, oils or other materials that may be hazardous in the work area, on the floor, or under vehicles that are not necessary.		
	III	Is the work area free of unnecessary items and tools?	Are items that are not needed been removed from the work zone, i.e. tools, parts, cans, tags, extra items.		
	IV	Is the work area free of excess consumables/materials?	Evaluate against how many items are in the work area. Assess if the materials, parts, and supplies are currently needed for the repair area, staging area, point area, etc.		
	V	Is the production/ information board active and to what degree?	All jobs in each respective area of the shop are known and displayed. Announcements are current and in presentable shape. Arrangement is straight and placed under appropriate headings.		
	VI	Are the area's walls and dividers free of items not used in the shop?	Extra items are not on the walls, dividers, or hanging of signs that are not necessary.		
			Category Subtotal		
			Sort Score: Subtotal divided by 6		
SET IN ORDER / STRAIGHTEN	VII	Evaluate any documentation storage.	Only documents to do the job are stored at the work area. Stock is limited and pre-staging is based on known lead-times throughput of the repair shop. Documentation is understandable to outsiders.		
	VIII	How are the shelves, desks, and work surfaces arranged?	All locations of items are labeled, marked, and it is known if they are missing.		
	IX	How are the tools and material used in operations stored?	No items are resting on or under automobiles nor tucked in corners. No items are resting on essential equipment, unknown in cupboards, or other places.		
	X	Evaluate temporary storage containers and staging locations and tidiness.	Parts, re-manufactured, components, and other items are stored in the appropriate place and orientated well for specific stage of the repair process. Items are secure and not causing any danger to the works.		
	XI	Assess orderliness of items on the shop's floor.	Minimal items are sitting directly on the floor and no materials are left around the vehicles. Items that need to be set on the floor are clearly marked and positioned in designated areas clearly outlined.		
	XII	Availability of tools for repair and teardown as well as measuring gauges.	Tools, components, measuring devices, and any fixtures need for teardown and repair are organized in a systematic way to ensure they are easily within reach and if not available are known where they are.		
			Category Subtotal		
			Set in Order / Straighten Score: Subtotal divided by 6		
SHINE / SWEEP	XIII	The storage of gauges and tooling.	Arrangement and storage of all fixtures, tools, and gauges are kept in clean well organized and visual area for storage and no risk of damage or loss can occur.		
	XIV	Clear when equipment needs maintenance and when last maintained.	Machines are clearly marked, highlighted, and labeled. Compliance or check sheets are clean and displayed. Any maintenance is known scheduled; fluid levels, lubrication, and joints are accessible.		
	XV	In each department assess the cleanliness of the work area.	How dust free are the areas. Look under equipment, under vehicles, behind work benches, and tool chests to see if there is garbage and other unnecessary items.		
	XVI	Safety, are areas sectioned off and safe for workers?	Spray shields and physical guards are in active use to keep paint overspray and other sprays within the department. How much paint is getting on the floor. All critical areas are clearly marked to protect workers.		
	XVII	Assess status of equipment in the area. Cleanliness overall appearance.	Are machines, repair equipment, and other vehicles known to be on a maintenance schedule for cleaning and repair?		
			Category Subtotal		
			Shine / Sweep Score: Subtotal divided by 5		
STANDARDIZE	XVIII	Is there visual color diagramming and color coding?	A clear and present color coding system is present in the work areas and across the shop. It's immediately clear that standards are being maintained and improved on.		
	XIX	Assess the access ways in case of emergency.	All emergency systems; fire vehicles, fire extinguishers, and emergency equipment free of obstruction and clear at all times. Access to electrical controls and fuses are known, marked, and free of any obstructions.		
	XX	The aisle ways are bright with light and clearly marked.	Walkways are clearly highlighted for direction, aisle access identified at any moment while in the work area. Transitional areas between the different departments and intersections are clearly marked.		
	XXI	General area has quantity limits for stored parts and are marked clearly.	Heights are marked, quantity of materials are known, and min vs. max is maintained. Shop carts are standardized to hold only parts for one vehicle. Large parts are clearly related to their respective cart.		
	XXII	Is there clear document control of information in the work zone?	All information and documentation is controlled, labeled, and revisions are up to date. There are no label-less binders or work orders in the area.		
			Category Subtotal		
			Standardize Score: Subtotal divided by 5		
SUSTAIN	XXIII	The aisle ways are clean and maintenance is clear.	Aisles are never full of anything and are clear for passage. All vehicle parts are stored in work areas and only in designated storage areas next to aisles therefore allowing accessible movement in the area.		
	XXIV	Illustrations and work area plans are available to compare against.	5S operates a system that allows for controlled change and further improvement of 5S in the work areas. Scoring is kept on each of these 5's and history is present and visible to support future improvement.		
	XXV	Organization is now visible. Tool locations are known and allocated.	No self-discipline is necessary to ensure that all tools, equipment, gauges, and parts are put back in the same spot. No extra effort is needed to sustain 5S in the area.		
	XXVI	Evaluate the involvement of supervisors in 5S.	Supervisors are actively involved in the review process of 5S and are supporting improvement activities of the work areas.		
			Category Subtotal		
			Sustain Score: Subtotal divided by 4		

Total "Category Subtotals" divide by 26 average 5S score: TOTAL [_____]

Auto Body — 5S Audit Review Form

Date: _____   Evaluation Area: _____

5S Element	Number	Evaluation Criteria	Rank these items from 1 through 5: 5 being well done	Score (1-5)	Ideas / Suggestions / Comments
SORT	I	Are the aisles and walkways open and clear?	All items that are not necessary or unsafe have been removed from the area where people travel and work.		
	II	Is the work area free of any spills of fluids?	Consider whether there are any lubricants, water, oils or other materials that may be hazardous in the work area, on the floor, or under vehicles that are not necessary.		
	III	Is the work area free of unnecessary items and tools?	Are items that are not needed been removed from the work zone, i.e. tools, parts, cans, tags, extra items.		
	IV	Is the work area free of excess consumables/materials?	Evaluate against how many items are in the work area. Assess if the materials, parts, and supplies are currently needed for the repair area, staging area, point area, etc.		
	V	Is the production/ information board active and to what degree?	All jobs in each respective area of the shop are known and displayed. Announcements are current and in presentable shape. Arrangement is straight and placed under appropriate headings.		
	VI	Are the area's walls and dividers free of items not used in the shop?	Extra items are not on the walls, dividers, or hanging of signs that are not necessary.		
			Category Subtotal		
			Sort Score: Subtotal divided by 6		
SET IN ORDER / STRAIGHTEN	VII	Evaluate any documentation storage.	Only documents to do the job are stored at the work area. Stock is limited and pre-staging is based on known lead-times throughput of the repair shop. Documentation is understandable to outsiders.		
	VIII	How are the shelves, desks, and work surfaces arranged?	All locations of items are labeled, marked, and it is known if they are missing.		
	IX	How are the tools and material used in operations stored?	No items are resting on or under automobiles nor tucked in corners. No items are resting on essential equipment, unknown in cupboards, or other places.		
	X	Evaluate temporary storage containers and staging locations and tidiness.	Parts, re-manufactured, components, and other items are stored in the appropriate place and orientated well for specific stage of the repair process. Items are secure and not causing any danger to the works.		
	XI	Assess orderliness of items on the shop's floor.	Minimal items are sitting directly on the floor and no materials are left around the vehicles. Items that need to be set on the floor are clearly marked and positioned in designated areas clearly outlined.		
	XII	Availability of tools for repair and teardown as well as measuring gauges.	Tools, components, measuring devices, and any fixtures need for teardown and repair are organized in a systematic way to ensure they are easily within reach and if not available are known where they are.		
			Category Subtotal		
			Set in Order / Straighten Score: Subtotal divided by 6		
SHINE / SWEEP	XIII	The storage of gauges and tooling.	Arrangement and storage of all fixtures, tools, and gauges are kept in clean well organized and visual area for storage and no risk of damage or loss can occur.		
	XIV	Clear when equipment needs maintenance and when last maintained.	Machines are clearly marked, highlighted, and labeled. Compliance or check sheets are clean and displayed. Any maintenance is known scheduled; fluid levels, lubrication, and joints are accessible.		
	XV	In each department assess the cleanliness of the work area.	How dust free are the areas. Look under equipment, under vehicles, behind work benches, and tool chests to see if there is garbage and other unnecessary items.		
	XVI	Safety, are areas sectioned off and safe for workers?	Spray shields and physical guards are in active use to keep paint overspray and other sprays within the department. How much paint is getting on the floor. All critical areas are clearly marked to protect workers.		
	XVII	Assess status of equipment in the area. Cleanliness overall appearance.	Are machines, repair equipment, and other vehicles known to be on a maintenance schedule for cleaning and repair?		
			Category Subtotal		
			Shine / Sweep Score: Subtotal divided by 5		
STANDARDIZE	XVIII	Is there visual color diagramming and color coding?	A clear and present color coding system is present in the work areas and across the shop. It's immediately clear that standards are being maintained and improved on.		
	XIX	Assess the access ways in case of emergency.	All emergency systems; fire vehicles, fire extinguishers, and emergency equipment free of obstruction and clear at all times. Access to electrical controls and fuses are known, marked, and free of any obstructions.		
	XX	The aisle ways are bright with light and clearly marked.	Walkways are clearly highlighted for direction, aisle access identified at any moment while in the work area. Transitional areas between the different departments and intersections are clearly marked.		
	XXI	General area has quantity limits for stored parts and are marked clearly.	Heights are marked, quantity of materials are known, and min vs. max is maintained. Shop carts are standardized to hold one parts for one vehicle. Large parts are clearly related to their respective cart.		
	XXII	Is there clear document control of information in the work zone?	All information and documentation is controlled, labeled, and revisions are up to date. There are no label-less binders or work orders in the area.		
			Category Subtotal		
			Standardize Score: Subtotal divided by 5		
SUSTAIN	XXIII	The aisle ways are clean and maintenance is clear.	Aisles are never full of anything and are clear for passage. All vehicle parts are stored in work areas and only in designated storage areas next to aisles therefore allowing accessible movement in the area.		
	XXIV	Illustrations and work area plans are available to compare against.	5S operates a system that allows for controlled change and further improvement of 5S in the work areas. Scoring is kept on each of these 5's and history is present and visible to support future improvement.		
	XXV	Organization is now visible. Tool locations are known and allocated.	No self-discipline is necessary to ensure that all tools, equipment, gauges, and parts are put back in the same spot. No extra effort is needed to sustain 5S in the area.		
	XXVI	Evaluate the involvement of supervisors in 5S.	Supervisors are actively involved in the review process of 5S and are supporting improvement activities of the work areas.		
			Category Subtotal		
			Sustain Score: Subtotal divided by 4		

Total "Category Subtotals" divide by 26 average 5S score: TOTAL [___]

Auto Body — 5S Audit Review Form

Date: _____   Evaluation Area: _____

5S Element	Number	Evaluation Criteria	Rank these items from 1 through 5: 5 being well done	Score (1-5)	Ideas / Suggestions / Comments
SORT	I	Are the aisles and walkways open and clear?	All items that are not necessary or unsafe have been removed from the area where people travel and work.		
	II	Is the work area free of any spills of fluids?	Consider whether there are any lubricants, water, oils or other materials that may be hazardous in the work area, on the floor, or under vehicles that are not necessary.		
	III	Is the work area free of unnecessary items and tools?	Are items that are not needed been removed from the work zone, i.e. tools, parts, cans, tags, extra items.		
	IV	Is the work area free of excess consumables/materials?	Evaluate against how many items are in the work area. Assess if the materials, parts, and supplies are currently needed for the repair area, staging area, point area, etc.		
	V	Is the production/ information board active and to what degree?	All jobs in each respective area of the shop are known and displayed. Announcements are current and in presentable shape. Arrangement is straight and placed under appropriate headings.		
	VI	Are the area's walls and dividers free of items not used in the shop?	Extra items are not on the walls, dividers, or hanging of signs that are not necessary.		
			Category Subtotal		
			Sort Score: Subtotal divided by 6		
SET IN ORDER / STRAIGHTEN	VII	Evaluate any documentation storage.	Only documents to do the job are stored at the work area. Stock is limited and pre-staging is based on known lead-times throughput of the repair shop. Documentation is understandable to outsiders.		
	VIII	How are the shelves, desks, and work surfaces arranged?	All locations of items are labeled, marked, and it is known if they are missing.		
	IX	How are the tools and material used in operations stored?	No items are resting on or under automobiles nor tucked in corners. No items are resting on essential equipment, unknown in cupboards, or other places.		
	X	Evaluate temporary storage containers and staging locations and tidiness.	Parts, re-manufactured, components, and other items are stored in the appropriate place and orientated well for specific stage of the repair process. Items are secure and not causing any danger to the works.		
	XI	Assess orderliness of items on the shop's floor.	Minimal items are sitting directly on the floor and no materials are left around the vehicles. Items that need to be set on the floor are clearly marked and positioned in designated areas clearly outlined.		
	XII	Availability of tools for repair and teardown as well as measuring gauges.	Tools, components, measuring devices, and any fixtures need for teardown and repair are organized in a systematic way to ensure they are easily within reach and if not available are known where they are.		
			Category Subtotal		
			Set in Order / Straighten Score: Subtotal divided by 6		
SHINE / SWEEP	XIII	The storage of gauges and tooling.	Arrangement and storage of all fixtures, tools, and gauges are kept in clean well organized and visual area for storage and no risk of damage or loss can occur.		
	XIV	Clear when equipment needs maintenance and when last maintained.	Machines are clearly marked, highlighted, and labeled. Compliance or check sheets are clean and displayed. Any maintenance is known scheduled; fluid levels, lubrication, and joints are accessible.		
	XV	In each department assess the cleanliness of the work area.	How dust free are the areas. Look under equipment, under vehicles, behind work benches, and tool chests to see if there is garbage and other unnecessary items.		
	XVI	Safety, are areas sectioned off and safe for workers?	Spray shields and physical guards are in active use to keep paint overspray and other sprays within the department. How much paint is getting on the floor. All critical areas are clearly marked to protect workers.		
	XVII	Assess status of equipment in the area. Cleanliness overall appearance.	Are machines, repair equipment, and other vehicles known to be on a maintenance schedule for cleaning and repair?		
			Category Subtotal		
			Shine / Sweep Score: Subtotal divided by 5		
STANDARDIZE	XVIII	Is there visual color diagramming and color coding?	A clear and present color coding system is present in the work areas and across the shop. It's immediately clear that standards are being maintained and improved on.		
	XIX	Assess the access ways in case of emergency.	All emergency systems; fire vehicles, fire extinguishers, and emergency equipment free of obstruction and clear at all times. Access to electrical controls and fuses are known, marked, and free of any obstructions.		
	XX	The aisle ways are bright with light and clearly marked.	Walkways are clearly highlighted for direction, aisle access identified at any moment while in the work area. Transitional areas between the different departments and intersections are clearly marked.		
	XXI	General area has quantity limits for stored parts and are marked clearly.	Heights are marked, quantity of materials are known, and min vs. max is maintained. Shop carts are standardized to hold only parts for one vehicle. Large parts are clearly related to their respective cart.		
	XXII	Is there clear document control of information in the work zone?	All information and documentation is controlled, labeled, and revisions are up to date. There are no label-less binders or work orders in the area.		
			Category Subtotal		
			Standardize Score: Subtotal divided by 5		
SUSTAIN	XXIII	The aisle ways are clean and maintenance is clear.	Aisles are never full of anything and are clear for passage. All vehicle parts are stored in work areas and only in designated storage areas next to aisles therefore allowing accessible movement in the area.		
	XXIV	Illustrations and work area plans are available to compare against.	5S operates a system that allows for controlled change and further improvement of 5S in the work areas. Scoring is kept on each of these 5's and history is present and visible to support future improvement.		
	XXV	Organization is now visible. Tool locations are known and allocated.	No self-discipline is necessary to ensure that all tools, equipment, gauges, and parts are put back in the same spot. No extra effort is needed to sustain 5S in the area.		
	XXVI	Evaluate the involvement of supervisors in 5S.	Supervisors are actively involved in the review process of 5S and are supporting improvement activities of the work areas.		
			Category Subtotal		
			Sustain Score: Subtotal divided by 4		**Total "Category Subtotals" divide by 26 average 5S score: TOTAL**

Auto Body — 5S Audit Review Form

Date: _____   Evaluation Area: _____

5S Element	Number	Evaluation Criteria	Rank these items from 1 through 5: 5 being well done	Score (1-5)	Ideas / Suggestions / Comments
SORT	I	Are the aisles and walkways open and clear?	All items that are not necessary or unsafe have been removed from the area where people travel and work.		
	II	Is the work area free of any spills of fluids?	Consider whether there are any lubricants, water, oils or other materials that may be hazardous in the work area, on the floor, or under vehicles that are not necessary.		
	III	Is the work area free of unnecessary items and tools?	Are items that are not needed been removed from the work zone, i.e. tools, parts, cans, tags, extra items.		
	IV	Is the work area free of excess consumables/materials?	Evaluate against how many items are in the work area. Assess if the materials, parts, and supplies are currently needed for the repair area, staging area, point area, etc.		
	V	Is the production/ information board active and to what degree?	All jobs in each respective area of the shop are known and displayed. Announcements are current and in presentable shape. Arrangement is straight and placed under appropriate headings.		
	VI	Are the area's walls and dividers free of items not used in the shop?	Extra items are not on the walls, dividers, or hanging of signs that are not necessary.		
			Category Subtotal		
			Sort Score: Subtotal divided by 6		
SET IN ORDER / STRAIGHTEN	VII	Evaluate any documentation storage.	Only documents to do the job are stored at the work area. Stock is limited and pre-staging is based on known lead-times throughput of the repair shop. Documentation is understandable to outsiders.		
	VIII	How are the shelves, desks, and work surfaces arranged?	All locations of items are labeled, marked, and it is known if they are missing.		
	IX	How are the tools and material used in operations stored?	No items are resting on or under automobiles nor tucked in corners. No items are resting on essential equipment, unknown in cupboards, or other places.		
	X	Evaluate temporary storage containers and staging locations and tidiness.	Parts, re-manufactured, components, and other items are stored in the appropriate place and orientated well for specific stage of the repair process. Items are secure and not causing any danger to the works.		
	XI	Assess orderliness of items on the shop's floor.	Minimal items are sitting directly on the floor and no materials are left around the vehicles. Items that need to be set on the floor are clearly marked and positioned in designated areas clearly outlined.		
	XII	Availability of tools for repair and teardown as well as measuring gauges.	Tools, components, measuring devices, and any fixtures need for teardown and repair are organized in a systematic way to ensure they are easily within reach and if not available are known where they are.		
			Category Subtotal		
			Set in Order / Straighten Score: Subtotal divided by 6		
SHINE / SWEEP	XIII	The storage of gauges and tooling.	Arrangement and storage of all fixtures, tools, and gauges are kept in clean well organized and visual area for storage and no risk of damage or loss can occur.		
	XIV	Clear when equipment needs maintenance and when last maintained.	Machines are clearly marked, highlighted, and labeled. Compliance or check sheets are clean and displayed. Any maintenance is known scheduled; fluid levels, lubrication, and joints are accessible.		
	XV	In each department assess the cleanliness of the work area.	How dust free are the areas. Look under equipment, under vehicles, behind work benches, and tool chests to see if there is garbage and other unnecessary items.		
	XVI	Safety, are areas sectioned off and safe for workers?	Spray shields and physical guards are in active use to keep paint overspray and other sprays within the department. How much paint is getting on the floor. All critical areas are clearly marked to protect workers.		
	XVII	Assess status of equipment in the area. Cleanliness overall appearance.	Are machines, repair equipment, and other vehicles known to be on a maintenance schedule for cleaning and repair?		
			Category Subtotal		
			Shine / Sweep Score: Subtotal divided by 5		
STANDARDIZE	XVIII	Is there visual color diagramming and color coding?	A clear and present color coding system is present in the work areas and across the shop. It's immediately clear that standards are being maintained and improved on.		
	XIX	Assess the access ways in case of emergency.	All emergency systems; fire vehicles, fire extinguishers, and emergency equipment free of obstruction and clear at all times. Access to electrical controls and fuses are known, marked, and free of any obstructions.		
	XX	The aisle ways are bright with light and clearly marked.	Walkways are clearly highlighted for direction, aisle access identified at any moment while in the work area. Transitional areas between the different departments and intersections are clearly marked.		
	XXI	General area has quantity limits for stored parts and are marked clearly.	Heights are marked, quantity of materials are known, and min vs. max is maintained. Shop carts are standardized to hold only parts for one vehicle. Large parts are clearly related to their respective cart.		
	XXII	Is there clear document control of information in the work zone?	All information and documentation is controlled, labeled, and revisions are up to date. There are no label-less binders or work orders in the area.		
			Category Subtotal		
			Standardize Score: Subtotal divided by 5		
SUSTAIN	XXIII	The aisle ways are clean and maintenance is clear.	Aisles are never full of anything and are clear for passage. All vehicle parts are stored in work areas and only in designated storage areas next to aisles therefore allowing accessible movement in the area.		
	XXIV	Illustrations and work area plans are available to compare against.	5S operates a system that allows for controlled change and further improvement of 5S in the work areas. Scoring is kept on each of these 5's and history is present and visible to support future improvement.		
	XXV	Organization is now visible. Tool locations are known and allocated.	No self-discipline is necessary to ensure that all tools, equipment, gauges, and parts are put back in the same spot. No extra effort is needed to sustain 5S in the area.		
	XXVI	Evaluate the involvement of supervisors in 5S.	Supervisors are actively involved in the review process of 5S and are supporting improvement activities of the work areas.		
			Category Subtotal		
			Sustain Score: Subtotal divided by 4		

Total "Category Subtotals" divide by 26 average 5S score: TOTAL _____

Auto Body 5S Audit Review Form

Date: _____   Evaluation Area: _____

5S Element	Number	Evaluation Criteria	Rank these items from 1 through 5: 5 being well done	Score (1-5)	Ideas / Suggestions / Comments
SORT	I	Are the aisles and walkways open and clear?	All items that are not necessary or unsafe have been removed from the area where people travel and work.		
	II	Is the work area free of any spills of fluids?	Consider whether there are any lubricants, water, oils or other materials that may be hazardous in the work area, on the floor, or under vehicles that are not necessary.		
	III	Is the work area free of unnecessary items and tools?	Are items that are not needed been removed from the work zone, i.e. tools, parts, cans, tags, extra items.		
	IV	Is the work area free of excess consumables/materials?	Evaluate against how many items are in the work area. Assess if the materials, parts, and supplies are currently needed for the repair area, staging area, point area, etc.		
	V	Is the production/ information board active and to what degree?	All jobs in each respective area of the shop are known and displayed. Announcements are current and in presentable shape. Arrangement is straight and placed under appropriate headings.		
	VI	Are the area's walls and dividers free of items not used in the shop?	Extra items are not on the walls, dividers, or hanging of signs that are not necessary.		
		Category Subtotal			
		Sort Score: Subtotal divided by 6			
SET IN ORDER / STRAIGHTEN	VII	Evaluate any documentation storage.	Only documents to do the job are stored at the work area. Stock is limited and pre-staging is based on known lead-times throughput of the repair shop. Documentation is understandable to outsiders.		
	VIII	How are the shelves, desks, and work surfaces arranged?	All locations of items are labeled, marked, and it is known if they are missing.		
	IX	How are the tools and material used in operations stored?	No items are resting on or under automobiles nor tucked in corners. No items are resting on essential equipment, unknown in cupboards, or other places.		
	X	Evaluate temporary storage containers and staging locations and tidiness.	Parts, re-manufactured, components, and other items are stored in the appropriate place and orientated well for specific stage of the repair process. Items are secure and not causing any danger to the works.		
	XI	Assess orderliness of items on the shop's floor.	Minimal items are sitting directly on the floor and no materials are left around the vehicles. Items that need to be set on the floor are clearly marked and positioned in designated areas clearly outlined.		
	XII	Availability of tools for repair and teardown as well as measuring gauges.	Tools, components, measuring devices, and any fixtures need for teardown and repair are organized in a systematic way to ensure they are easily within reach and if not available are known where they are.		
		Category Subtotal			
		Set in Order / Straighten Score: Subtotal divided by 6			
SHINE / SWEEP	XIII	The storage of gauges and tooling.	Arrangement and storage of all fixtures, tools, and gauges are kept in clean well organized and visual area for storage and no risk of damage or loss can occur.		
	XIV	Clear when equipment needs maintenance and when last maintained.	Machines are clearly marked, highlighted, and labeled. Compliance or check sheets are clean and displayed. Any maintenance is known scheduled; fluid levels, lubrication, and joints are accessible.		
	XV	In each department assess the cleanliness of the work area.	How dust free are the areas. Look under equipment, under vehicles, behind work benches, and tool chests to see if there is garbage and other unnecessary items.		
	XVI	Safety, are areas sectioned off and safe for workers?	Spray shields and physical guards are in active use to keep paint overspray and other sprays within the department. How much paint is getting on the floor. All critical areas are clearly marked to protect workers.		
	XVII	Assess status of equipment in the area. Cleanliness overall appearance.	Are machines, repair equipment, and other vehicles known to be on a maintenance schedule for cleaning and repair?		
		Category Subtotal			
		Shine / Sweep Score: Subtotal divided by 5			
STANDARDIZE	XVIII	Is there visual color diagramming and color coding?	A clear and present color coding system is present in the work areas and across the shop. It's immediately clear that standards are being maintained and improved on.		
	XIX	Assess the access ways in case of emergency.	All emergency systems; fire vehicles, fire extinguishers, and emergency equipment free of obstruction and clear at all times. Access to electrical controls and fuses are known, marked, and free of any obstructions.		
	XX	The aisle ways are bright with light and clearly marked.	Walkways are clearly highlighted for direction, aisle access identified at any moment while in the work area. Transitional areas between the different departments and intersections are clearly marked.		
	XXI	General area has quantity limits for stored parts and are marked clearly.	Heights are marked, quantity of materials are known, and min vs. max is maintained. Shop carts are standardized to hold only parts for one vehicle. Large parts are clearly related to their respective cart.		
	XXII	Is there clear document control of information in the work zone?	All information and documentation is controlled, labeled, and revisions are up to date. There are no label-less binders or work orders in the area.		
		Category Subtotal			
		Standardize Score: Subtotal divided by 5			
SUSTAIN	XXIII	The aisle ways are clean and maintenance is clear.	Aisles are never full of anything and are clear for passage. All vehicle parts are stored in work areas and only in designated storage areas next to aisles therefore allowing accessible movement in the areas.		
	XXIV	Illustrations and work area plans are available to compare against.	5S operates a system that allows for controlled change and further improvement of 5S in the work areas. Scoring is kept on each of these 5's and history is present and visible to support future improvement.		
	XXV	Organization is now visible. Tool locations are known and allocated.	No self-discipline is necessary to ensure that all tools, equipment, gauges, and parts are put back in the same spot. No extra effort is needed to sustain 5S in the area.		
	XXVI	Evaluate the involvement of supervisors in 5S.	Supervisors are actively involved in the review process of 5S and are supporting improvement activities of the work areas.		
		Category Subtotal			
		Sustain Score: Subtotal divided by 4		Total "Category Subtotals" divide by 26 average 5S score: TOTAL	

Auto Body — 5S Audit Review Form

Date: _____   Evaluation Area: _____

5S Element	Number	Evaluation Criteria	Rank these items from 1 through 5: 5 being well done	Score (1-5)	Ideas / Suggestions / Comments
SORT	I	Are the aisles and walkways open and clear?	All items that are not necessary or unsafe have been removed from the area where people travel and work.		
	II	Is the work area free of any spills of fluids?	Consider whether there are any lubricants, water, oils or other materials that may be hazardous in the work area, on the floor, or under vehicles that are not necessary.		
	III	Is the work area free of unnecessary items and tools?	Are items that are not needed been removed from the work zone, i.e. tools, parts, cans, tags, extra items.		
	IV	Is the work area free of excess consumables/materials?	Evaluate against how many items are in the work area. Assess if the materials, parts, and supplies are currently needed for the repair area, staging area, point area, etc.		
	V	Is the production/ information board active and to what degree?	All jobs in each respective area of the shop are known and displayed. Announcements are current and in presentable shape. Arrangement is straight and placed under appropriate headings.		
	VI	Are the area's walls and dividers free of items not used in the shop?	Extra items are not on the walls, dividers, or hanging of signs that are not necessary.		

Category Subtotal _____

Sort Score: Subtotal divided by 6

5S Element	Number	Evaluation Criteria	Rank these items from 1 through 5: 5 being well done	Score (1-5)	Ideas / Suggestions / Comments
SET IN ORDER / STRAIGHTEN	VII	Evaluate any documentation storage.	Only documents to do the job are stored at the work area. Stock is limited and pre-staging is based on known lead-times throughout of the repair shop. Documentation is understandable to outsiders.		
	VIII	How are the shelves, desks, and work surfaces arranged?	All locations of items are labeled, marked, and it is known if they are missing.		
	IX	How are the tools and material used in operations stored?	No items are resting on or under automobiles nor tucked in corners. No items are resting on essential equipment, unknown in cupboards, or other places.		
	X	Evaluate temporary storage containers and staging locations and tidiness.	Parts, re-manufactured, components, and other items are stored in the appropriate place and orientated well for specific stage of the repair process. Items are secure and not causing any danger to the works.		
	XI	Assess orderliness of items on the shop's floor.	Minimal items are sitting directly on the floor and no materials are left around the vehicles. Items that need to be set on the floor are clearly marked and positioned in designated areas clearly outlined.		
	XII	Availability of tools for repair and teardown as well as measuring gauges.	Tools, components, measuring devices, and any fixtures need for teardown and repair are organized in a systematic way to ensure they are easily within reach and if not available are known where they are.		

Category Subtotal _____

Set in Order / Straighten Score: Subtotal divided by 6

5S Element	Number	Evaluation Criteria	Rank these items from 1 through 5: 5 being well done	Score (1-5)	Ideas / Suggestions / Comments
SHINE / SWEEP	XIII	The storage of gauges and tooling.	Arrangement and storage of all fixtures, tools, and gauges are kept in clean well organized and visual area for storage and no risk of damage or loss can occur.		
	XIV	Clear when equipment needs maintenance and when last maintained.	Machines are clearly marked, highlighted, and labeled. Compliance or check sheets are clean and displayed. Any maintenance is known scheduled; fluid levels, lubrication, and joints are accessible.		
	XV	In each department assess the cleanliness of the work area.	How dust free are the areas. Look under equipment, under vehicles, behind work benches, and tool chests to see if there is garbage and other unnecessary items.		
	XVI	Safety, are areas sectioned off and safe for workers?	Spray shields and physical guards are in active use to keep paint overspray and other sprays within the department. How much paint is getting on the floor. All critical areas are clearly marked to protect workers.		
	XVII	Assess status of equipment in the area. Cleanliness overall appearance.	Are machines, repair equipment, and other vehicles known to be on a maintenance schedule for cleaning and repair?		

Category Subtotal _____

Shine / Sweep Score: Subtotal divided by 5

5S Element	Number	Evaluation Criteria	Rank these items from 1 through 5: 5 being well done	Score (1-5)	Ideas / Suggestions / Comments
STANDARDIZE	XVIII	Is there visual color diagramming and color coding?	A clear and present color coding system is present in the work areas and across the shop. It's immediately clear that standards are being maintained and improved on.		
	XIX	Assess the access ways in case of emergency.	All emergency systems; fire vehicles, fire extinguishers, and emergency equipment free of obstruction and clear at all times. Access to electrical controls and fuses are known, marked, and free of any obstructions.		
	XX	The aisle ways are bright with light and clearly marked.	Walkways are clearly highlighted for direction, aisle access identified at any moment while in the work area. Transitional areas between the different departments and intersections are clearly marked.		
	XXI	General area has quantity limits for stored parts and are marked clearly.	Heights are marked, quantity of materials are known, and min vs. max is maintained. Shop carts are standardized to hold only parts for one vehicle. Large parts are clearly related to their respective cart.		
	XXII	Is there clear document control of information in the work zone?	All information and documentation is controlled, labeled, and revisions are up to date. There are no label-less binders or work orders in the area.		

Category Subtotal _____

Standardize Score: Subtotal divided by 5

5S Element	Number	Evaluation Criteria	Rank these items from 1 through 5: 5 being well done	Score (1-5)	Ideas / Suggestions / Comments
SUSTAIN	XXIII	The aisle ways are clean and maintenance is clear.	Aisles are never full of anything and are clear for passage. All vehicle parts are stored in work areas and only in designated storage areas next to aisles therefore allowing accessible movement in the area.		
	XXIV	Illustrations and work area plans are available to compare against.	5S operates a system that allows for controlled change and further improvement of 5S in the work areas. Scoring is kept on each of these 5's and history is present and visible to support future improvement.		
	XXV	Organization is now visible. Tool locations are known and allocated.	No self-discipline is necessary to ensure that all tools, equipment, gauges, and parts are put back in the same spot. No extra effort is needed to sustain 5S in the area.		
	XXVI	Evaluate the involvement of supervisors in 5S.	Supervisors are actively involved in the review process of 5S and are supporting improvement activities of the work areas.		

Category Subtotal _____

Sustain Score: Subtotal divided by 4

Total "Category Subtotals" divide by 26 average 5S score: TOTAL _____